The Silent Tranformations

THE FRENCH LIST

The Silent Tranformations

FRANÇOIS JULLIEN

TRANSLATED BY
MICHAEL RICHARDSON
AND KRZYSZTOF FIJALKOWSKI

LONDON NEW YORK CALCUTTA

Seagull Books 2011

François Jullien, *Les Transformations Silencieuses*
© Grasset & Fasquelle, 2009

English translation
© Michael Richardson and Krzysztof Fijalkowski 2011

ISBN-13   978 1 9064 9 787 3

British Library Cataloguing-in-Publication Data
A catalogue record for this book is available from the British Library

Typeset and designed by Seagull Books, Calcutta, India
Printed and bound by Hyam Enterprises, Calcutta, India

CONTENTS

6

Chapter 1
From Another Perspective than
the Subject-Action/Transformation

16

Chapter 2
Beneath the Transformation—
the Transition

25

Chapter 3
The Snow Melts
(Or How the Bias of Being Prevents us from
Thinking about the Transition)

41

Chapter 4
Do Modifications have a Beginning?

52

Chapter 5
Transition or Crossing—
Ageing has Always Already Started

Chapter 6
Figures of Reversal

Chapter 7
The Fluidity of Life
(Or How One is Already the Other)

Chapter 8
Was it Necessary to Invent 'Time'?

Chapter 9
Mythology of the Event

Chapter 10
Of the Concept which is Lacking—
Historical-Strategic-Political

Bibliography

Index

To Pierre Jullien,
careful observer of silent transformations.

10 August 2008

Why is it that all that tirelessly occurs in front of us, that functions in such an effective way and is also obvious, remains unseen?

Certainly it is effective: so much so that an effect of the real, in the end, makes itself brutally felt and hits us full in the face. Because it is not a question here of an internal, secret, psychological invisibility, one of the feelings; nor is it about the invisibility of ideas; that philosophy has decreed from the first an essence other than the perceptible. No, the invisibility about which I am speaking is characteristic of the 'phenomenon' and forms its paradox: what is continually produced and manifested most openly before us—but so continually and globally—is not for all that easily discerned. It is discreet due to the fact that it occurs slowly while also being of too broad an extent to be distinguished. There is no sudden bedazzlement which would confuse the gaze by its sudden springing up; on the contrary, it is the most banal thing: what is everywhere and at all times offered to sight, by this very fact, is never perceived—only its results are noticed.

To grow—we do not see growth, whether we are looking at children or at trees. And yet one day when we see them again we are surprised at how the trunk has already become thick or that the child is so tall that he now comes up to our shoulder. To age: we do not see ageing. This is not just because we are continually ageing, and in a way that is too progressive and continuous to be apparent to our eyes, but also because everything within us ages. Everything: not only does our hair turn grey, but also bags form under our eyes, lines grow thicker, our features become heavier, our shape is weighed down and the face becomes 'like plaster'. In addition the complexion changes, the skin cracks, the flesh sinks and retracts and so on. I'll say no more; it has been described for such a long time in all of the literatures of the world, with irony or with pity; and also, no matter how much one enumerates this, it will never approach the totality. 'The totality' means that nothing escapes: the gaze grows old and so do the smile and the timbre of the voice and the articulation of the hands—everything bends as of course does our 'bearing' with its leaden shoes attached to the feet, as Proust said.

Now, because it is the *whole* that is modified, and that nothing can be isolated from it, what is clearly in becoming, and is even displayed before our eyes, is not seen. Perhaps one morning some premonitory grey hairs have been located on the temple. But all in all they have only an anecdotal presence. Because it is not grey hairs which give you the appearance of being old and that one day causes people to get up to offer you their seat on the bus. No, it is 'air'; in other words it's everything, it's everywhere ... Don't those who place their trust in plastic surgery know something about it? When they repair the ageing at the corner of the eyes or on their face, they make it more glaringly obvious, by contrast, in their bent back and the faded timbre of their voice. Moreover those grey hairs are only an accidental, if a bit more prominent, sign of the 'silent transformation' we do not see in operation.

In fact, 'silent' is a more precise word to use in this respect than invisible, or rather it is more telling. Because not only is this transformation in process, even if we do not perceive it, but it operates without warning, without giving an alert, 'in silence' without attracting attention, and as though independently of us: without wanting to disturb us, it might be said, even when it continues on its way within us until it destroys us. Then one day we come across a photograph from twenty years earlier and we are suddenly seized with an irrepressible disturbance. The searching look is swallowed up in this question: How can that face be me? It is not 'me', but if it is not, then who can it be? Admittedly, by patiently recomposing the features I do gradually recognize myself, but only in an allusive and very strange way: under this perplexed gaze, the 'self' is undone. Equally, in coming across a friend one has not seen for several years: '... he had preserved many features of his former self. And yet I could not take it in that it was he' (Proust, at the end of *Time Regained*; see Proust 1981b: 314).

In evoking it at will, as in the last morning at the home of the Princess of Guermantes, literature takes its revenge on philosophy because it makes apparent what (European) philosophy has not considered. Philosophy has left aside this gaping hole that suddenly arises in our experience. Admittedly I know it, when I come across that friend or when I look at this photograph (that it is him, that it is me), but at the same time I do not believe it. Not that I have any doubt about it (the well known 'doubt' which is inserted into philosophy), but how can I manage to accept it and convince myself of its reality? What breach has then opened up between the two which reason is unable to put back together? So what density—or density of what?—creates the resistance here? Let's even confess that the question which then arises and keeps us perplexed appears to us to lead to a quite different possible question—with it we begin to draw a thread, in the anodyne, the everyday, which, one senses, already risks carrying us too far astray. But at root would this question be the only important one? It is clear, in any case, that it suddenly bores into a completely different depth, or radicalism, than do the others: opening out onto the unexpected, as if inadvertently, that it is a greater truth than any other truth—the most exposed, baldest and least effusive question.

There really is 'revelation' here, as they say, arising in this indentation but which has nothing to do, this time, with mystical solicitation, so much is that obvious thing which then appears before us really the only one that is unchallengeable and is even on the point of carrying everything into its vertigo. 'I have aged'—but is one word enough to say it? Or is not this word more 'vulgar' than all other words? Because until now silent, the transformation imposes itself in the most glaring way, so much more brutal, in its results, and this effect of the real really hits us full in the face. Here then is what operates so mutely within me—to the point that there is no longer a 'me'—and which has nevertheless eluded my consciousness; and suddenly casts so distantly from us—as though they were so abstract and secondary—the well-known problems of knowledge in which philosophy takes pleasure.

Chapter 1

FROM ANOTHER PERSPECTIVE
THAN THE SUBJECT-ACTION/TRANSFORMATION

For the sake of convenience, I will first of all go back to the rival terms between which contemporary philosophy is divided in order to explicate in a more unhurried way my surprise (when faced with the photograph of twenty years earlier): it would be of a 'subject' which finds itself to be a 'process' and one in which it sees itself immersed—absorbed. I thought I was a *subject*: a subject of initiative, one who conceives and desires, is active or passive, but one which always retains the sense of its being and self-possession. Admittedly it is a self that knows itself to be caught in a totality of external as well as internal interactions which hem it in, but it still considers itself to be 'generated from within', according to the expression dear to metaphysics, *causa sui*. And then, right in front of me, this perspective is suddenly violently shaken, capsizing into this otherness:

that of a cause or a *continuum* whose sole consistency stems from a mutual correlation of factors—mutually maintained and without regard to 'me'—and from which this evolution of the whole proceeds without interruption in an obvious but imperceptible way. 'I' am this (the) 'ageing'. Because ageing is not simply a property or an attribute of my being, or even a gradual alteration brought to constancy and stability; it is really a consistent sequence, one that is global and self-unfolding, of which the 'I' is the successive product. It may even be nothing but the convenient indicator of this sequence. Faced with the photograph of twenty years earlier, it is this validity of the 'subject' which suddenly falters. For all that we cannot say that the notion of it is false, that it necessarily abandons its option of autonomy and Liberty, only that its pertinence is suddenly found to be limited. Suddenly, faced with this vestige from twenty years earlier, it has all too easily recovered an other which has brutally resurfaced and created a sense of vertigo.

While making a claim for 'non-action' and the withdrawal of such a subject setting itself up in theory, a different tradition of thought, like that of the Chinese, in contrast makes us aware of the intelligibility which suddenly we appear to lack. In any case it furnishes us with an initial angle from which to locate ourselves within this disarray. It is a displacement that can be useful to us because, far from advocating disengagement or passivity in relation to this question, it valorizes transformation in the face of action, and it does so in the very name of what is *effective*. Are the two not in fact diametrically opposed? *Action* is localized and momentary (even if this moment may last), and it intervenes here and now, *hic et nunc*, really referring back to a subject as well as to its author (which can be plural). It is consequently differentiated from the course of things and stands out; therefore we notice it: we see the subject act, can trace its narrative—the epic. Inversely we notice that in Chinese thought *transformation* is global, progressive and situated in duration, resulting from a correlation of factors. Since 'everything' within it transforms itself, it is never sufficiently differentiated to be perceptible (see Jullien 2004, Chapter 4). We do not see the wheat ripen, but we do notice its result: when it is ripe and should be cut.

To put it bluntly, there is even an inversion between Greek and Chinese thought in this respect, and the latter opens up an initial breach—offers us an initia engagement—along a path of analysis that has barely been marked out. Because on the one hand Aristotelian nature, the *phusis*, is conceived as being a subject-agent: it 'wants', 'aims', 'undertakes', is 'ingenious' and sets up 'goals'. The Chinese sage or strategist, on the other hand, displays no other ambition than to 'transform' just as nature does (*hua* is their master word). The strategist transforms the relation of forces in such a way as to cause it to swing silently to his advantage within duration: combat will then no sooner have begun than the adversary will fall of his own accord, unable to resist and already defeated. As for the Sage (or the Prince), far from claiming to give lessons or impose orders, through direct signs, or wanting to impress others through miracles and exploits, he will be content with gradually 'transforming' the behaviour of those around him in silence: indeed, as the days go by, just the example of his conduct in itself extends from him and *influences*; due to this fact alone and through the impact it makes, it imperceptibly impregnates and modifies behaviour—it is all that is needed in order to educate. Since his example circulates without any planned intention but, rather, by contamination, across his domain and spreads like a stain, his range extends inexhaustibly—by self-deployment and without encountering resistance—out from his family across the land, we are told, and to the ends of the earth.

Instead of claiming to 'act', which also means having to take risks, to confront and to wear down, since, when all is said and done, this epiphenomenon of action has so little effect, 'transformation' occurs as it does in nature. But of course, since what is gradually modified through the effects of the environment, from near to far, is 'everything', we discern nothing of it, and as a result have nothing to describe or recount about it. Your efforts will not be celebrated; no sagas or epics,

For all that, is this discreet influence—which will be distilled from one day to the next—not finally more effective, as Chinese literature never tires of repeating, than all the might and noise made by dint of heroic action or prescriptions of 'Salvation'? (See, for example, the *Zhongyong*, § 11.) Because it is everywhere, in all things, that the results of this beneficial process will be measured, this prevailing conditioning is shown better in 'habits', *mores*, than in the individual morality and choices made by the Subject. And will not these results even be perceived in the serene and confident tunes one hears being sung by ordinary folk, free of complaint and forming the 'ambiance' of a land (*guo-feng*), by the people of the nation, reflections of those peaceful times, spreading with confidence and harmony during the course of their daily work? There is admittedly nothing spectacular and heroic in that. But this is what has been read, over two millennia, in the most ancient literature of China, the *Classic of Poems* (*Shijing*), which is the equivalent of our epics, the Odyssey and the Iliad (see Jullien 2003, Chapter 3, §1: 91).

What other possibilities for coherence have we in Europe allowed to elude us, even though they have developed elsewhere, and which we should today start to recover? Having embarked and made its choice in favour of the Subject, action, and foremost of having metaphysically promoted the invisible to the level of the intelligible, Western reason appears to have suddenly been taken by surprise, as though naively at fault, when faced with these grand appeals to the order of nature. Is this not so—the theme of the day—in relation to global warming? And what is global warming if it is not also, par excellence and in a typified way, a 'silent transformation'? As we have not known how to give sufficient attention to this most *unassuming* of influences, which operates step by step, suddenly, and this time for all of us, it comes back to hit us right in the face. Or, rather, because we are not sufficiently alert to *ad hoc* categories of thinking about it, we have not until now known how to pay it proper attention. In fact, because this warming has been produced infinitesimally, in the course of days and seconds, because it has arisen from an indefinite number of factors, it cannot even be identified as a separate phenomenon, and because it is 'everything', on the earth, which is involved, we do not see the earth getting warmer. We no more see the world getting warmer than we see rivers carve out their beds, glaciers melt or the sea eat into the shore, and yet this is what is constantly happening in front of our eyes: what forms, wears away and smoothes all the folds of the scene and from one day to the next gives an outline to the landscape we see. For, returning to these places later, we measure how the glaciers have melted from here to there and that the desert silently has continued to advance.

Let's change the scene—the process is the same; we even see that this concept of silent transformation undermines the function of the Subject within the very heart of what would seem to be its foremost privilege: in the order of emotions and of psychology, that we thought belonged to it by rights and which formed its last bastion. A man and a woman 'no longer love one another'. What they had not earlier even been able to conceive has nevertheless really and truly happened: from that point they have no other choice than to break up. Once again, is not the rupture the result of a silent transformation which has ceaselessly been at work? Can they forget those first silences, those first avoidances, or even those first lighter touches which, as the days went by, and without it having occurred to them to do anything about it, have produced an affective erosion resembling the sort of geological erosion which suddenly causes a whole section of the cliff to collapse onto the shore? But, since it is 'everything' that is gradually modified between them and nothing escapes the process, since all these modifications (intonations, looks and gestures of impatience) go hand in hand to the point of inversion as in a well-ordered symphony, nothing is singled out and the pervasive evolution has remained as invisible to them as the air they breathe. Then one day, something even quite trivial happens, something purely anecdotal, and they are suddenly made to realize that their relationship is finished, that their sense of complicity has changed into one of indifference, or even intolerance, and that, in spite of the effort they still make to hide this evidence from themselves, they no longer have a common future ahead of them.

Pascal: 'He no longer loves the person whom he loved ten years ago. I quite believe it; she is not the same any more, nor is he. He was young, and so was she; now she is quite different. Perhaps he would love her still as she used to be then' (1966: 242). In fact, if Pascal makes a case from this observation in order to show that this fickleness is that of the self-subject which leads it, defeated, to turn towards God, it no less retains its dependency on it. Also, being unable to conceive of escaping this condition, he can only give a cursory explanation based purely on what results and so makes do with the change recorded. Moreover, is this simply a matter of lost 'youth'; do not elderly lovers exist? I rather think that, in order to understand this silent transformation which has led to disaffection, it would be necessary not only to overturn the perspective of the self-subject which suddenly finds that, ten years later, it has changed so much, into that perspective of a process of maturation, or rather of slow and global degradation; but equally to postpone what one might at first sight believe arose from the initiative of the subject, which Pascal simply divided into two (She and He), in favour of the situation involved which was, as such, given over to erosion. Or should one not even make this situation that unravels (destroys) the real subject? Are these two people effectively and personally to blame for the disaffection which touches them, or are the errors which they now pitilessly calculate against one another not, once again, nothing but an anecdotal orientation? Nothing is more vain than the complaints former lovers interminably make towards one another, as all of the evidence shows.

But what precisely is a *situation*, and to what extent does it overcome the subjects themselves—whom we thought came first? Will we be limited to the encounter in which one of them one day met someone else, triggering a new love, the moment that brought grief to the other one? But this encounter might itself be the result of only consequential factors: because progressively differences between the two existences had silently increased, differences between two vital rhythms and everyday occupations, which each one models in their own way, and so atavisms return . . . so preparing the ground for the opportunity, for the encounter with another person, who one day appears; or, worse still, for the solitary sinking of each of them into old age. Overnight the outline of a breach has become a fissure, a crack, a lack, a trench; the tiny has become infinite, so that 'everything' between them has become contaminated. The gap has widened, as they say, it has unfolded so as to result in this trench of indifference which suddenly amazes them and effects the divorce. Could this still be considered a *matter between subjects*? When, confronted with this evolution which has escaped them, they contrarily plead passivity and blame destiny, they are still wrong. Because is this not more simply (actually) the fact that the *situational* has prevailed over the *personal*, to the point that, as it has become between them, they now have hardly any control over this relationship? From that point on, what is the use of all the bouts of good will and laborious papering over of the cracks? To do so would be like trying to stop a flow of water (even if only of a narrow stream) with one's hands.

Chapter 2
BENEATH THE TRANSFORMATION—
THE TRANSITION

We should not allow ourselves to be deluded about the difficulty we encounter in thinking about the transformation which, on principle, I think, always remains 'silent'. This is not in fact just a question of a difference of scale and size because we would only be able to grasp what has happened in a general way and, because of this, only after the event, roughly, in fact only gradually and on an infinitely small scale; because, all in all, we would not have sufficiently keen sight or fine enough hearing to be able to distinguish what is microscopic. The difficulty in thinking about the transformation needs to be grasped at a much earlier stage and I think effectively means putting our finger on the precise point at which our (European) way of thinking is found to be wanting. This difficulty is that of thinking about the very being that has transition at its core, the transition which explicitly addresses, if I arrange one term below the other, the 'passage' permitting the movement from one 'form' to the next—in the *between-forms*, if I can call it this, and developing as best as one can this *trans* of 'transformation'. But, precisely because it is not part of 'being', the transition escapes our thought. On this precise point, our thought stops, it no longer has anything to say, it ceases to speak, and this is also why the transformation is necessarily considered 'silent'.

The *transition* literally bores a hole into European thought, reducing it to silence. In evidence we can take what Plato says, or rather does not say, about it (in relation to the *One* of *Parmenides*; see Plato 1961a, 155d–157a: 946–8). Because how, he wonders, can I pass from non-being to being, or from immobility to mobility? I am sitting, then I walk: how do I grasp this transition or this intervening period (*metaxu*) that the word 'then' is happy to suggest while retaining these two juxtaposed moments, which are completely external to one another, in a solely successive mode? Because, as Plato pronounces in a logical way, I am either sitting or walking, I am doing one or the other, and I cannot do both at the same time; neither can I be doing neither one nor the other: to be neither moving nor motionless. Consequently, would not what we are calling the transition be a contradiction in terms? Plato thus has no other solution than to keep the two moments, of before and after, strictly separate from one another: when I am contributing by moving, 'other is the time', and when I am not contributing to it, other is the time. But what happens *between* the two? Plato himself has no more logical solution to the passing from contiguity to continuity than to assume that between them is an instant which would be neither of one time nor of the other and would thus be, he concludes, 'outside of time'. In order to link one to the other, the before and the after, there therefore remains to him no other resource than to invent a sudden 'outside of time' (*exaiphnes*) which, as such, has effectively no possible 'place', is 'atopical' (so 'strange'!), and it brutally bores a hole into the continuity of the change.

In this I see less a weakness in Platonic thought as it pushes itself to its limits than a symptom. For could we believe that this black hole impinging on reflection about the transition affects Plato alone, entangled as he was in his theory of participation in ideal-Forms and of the separation of essences? Aristotle was quick to criticize him and we also know that, in contrast, the author of *Physics* was the thinker of change. But was Aristotle in a better position to think through the status of this 'between' of transition and passage? Let's consider, for example, the median note in music or grey among colours. Aristotle says about this median note that it 'is low relatively to the highest and high relatively to the lowest'; and in the same way, that grey 'is white relatively to black and black relatively to white' (1984a,

224b: 380). If therefore the change ensues from what is 'between' or intermediary, it is because the latter renews as much for its own sake, on a minor mode, the status of the *extreme* while serving anew as contrary to one or the other of the oppositions; or, as Aristotle sums up, 'this intermediary is in a certain way the extremes' (*to metaxu ta akra*), which both demarcate and take one or the other of them over. The intermediary is a middle term, but it is still a term and quite as much a *terminus*. It interrupts the change in mid-path and decomposes it while constituting itself at a point that is at once that of the arrival and departure of the change. But this understanding takes us no nearer to grasping how the passage operates through it.

'Grey' is therefore not grey, according to Aristotle; in other words, it is a colour through which one turns into another but which is no longer either one or the other: a colour in which white and black, as they are mixed, lose their point of demarcation; that can neither be divided nor distinguished—is 'indecisive', as Verlaine said. It is alternatively—but imperturbably—'white in relation to black and black in relation to white'. As with Plato, what holds Aristotle back from thinking about the *between* as between is that it lacks the determination which constitutes 'being'. Since it is not part of 'being', such is the Greek postulate, it cannot be blurred but must be distinct and determined. Or rather, since thinking cannot be envisaged otherwise than in terms of Being, this is more than a postulate; it is the habitual Greek way of thinking in which the *trans* of transformation is to be logically immersed, or rather denied, and it is this denial that I am bringing into question.

Would it not be the case that Aristotle and Plato were alike frightened by what would, in the indistinction of the transition, be the disappearance of the form-essence, the *eidos* which is also its *logos*, discourse-reason and which is the only thing within reality, as far as they could see, that maintained its consistency? Dreading what is absurd about this, Aristotle stumbled over what would, at once, be in the process of engendering and already engendered, yet still be without being. When he confronts this issue, his phraseology is confused and it becomes unreadable (ibid., 226a: 382). With what could it then approximate—but which precisely is not of the order of the 'what' of Being and of something—so as not be thrown into a panic? For all that it is already recognized, it is not within the thought of the 'beyond', in the bold construction of the *meta* of meta-physics and of going beyond, that Greek thought hesitates, but really in this hole left unexpectedly gaping between the two; or, if I have spoken earlier of it being a symptom, it is because, in a revelatory way, nothing less than all of this bias about Being and the great edifice which it calls 'ontological' is found to be faulty and beginning to leak due to the transition.

In truth, 'transition' appears to me to be a limited term, having become overused, which gives a literal indication of what is at issue but without allowing it to be considered further. By continuing to use this term, we will soon come to a dead end: how does one disengage from the thought of Being that can so obviously be seen to stumble here? Or again, in going back to the question: since it has passed Being aside, would not Chinese thought again offer us, by its divergence (*écart*), a convenient expedient by which to emerge again from this impasse? In fact it offers us not one term but two. These are 'modification-continuation' ('communication'), as the Chinese say (*bian-tong*), making a conjunction which allows us to use them dialectically. On the one hand, these two terms are opposed, the modification to the continuation: modification 'bifurcates' and continuation 'pursues', one of them is 'innovative' while the other 'inherits'. But on the other hand, and at the same time, each of the terms marks the condition of the other: it is thanks to 'modification' that the process in train does not exhaust itself but, being renewed by it, can 'continue'; and reciprocally it is continuity, or rather continuation, which allows 'communication' even through the 'modification' which arises and turns it too into a time of transition.

Let's take as an example the seasons, which have always inspired Chinese thought (*The Book of Changes, I Ching*[1]): the 'modification' occurs from winter to spring, or from summer to autumn, when the cold is reversed and tends towards warmth, or warmth towards cold; as for 'continuation', it manifests itself from spring to summer, or from autumn to winter, when warmth becomes warmer or the cold becomes colder. Each moment alternates, from modification or from continuation, but even that of the modification, as it corrects the factor which is wearing out by means of the other, functions in such a way as to benefit its other and so serves the continuation of the totality of the process. No breakdown could happen at the heart of this unfolding. Equally it is principally by reference to spring and autumn, seasons incarnating the transition and so exemplary of this continuation, that the Chinese have conceived the course of the year and named their ancient chronicles (*Chun-qiu*).

In order to emerge from the thought of Being, it will therefore be necessary to consider an earlier point in the thought of each of the thinkers, Greek and Chinese, and to investigate the biases that, anchored in language and anthropology, they elucidate. This means no longer posing the question of 'what is it?' or 'is it this or is it not this?', as the Greeks did in the beginning, from the perspective of an identification which would be speculative; but, in its way of rising towards the world and of tying up an initial agreement with it, by giving priority to the rhythm of the seasons as the bearers of regulation, approaching life by the respiration which renews it, and following the instructive way by which spring becomes summer without there being even the slightest separation between them. Or, from a logical point of view, as is already implicated in the sentence, to understand how the concession can go together with the consequence and again bring our disjunctive syntax into question: to understand how the same 'empty word' of the Chinese language (*er*) can mean both 'but' and 'in such a way that'. This is so much so that the same formula revolving around it (*bian er tong*) serves to translate at the same time 'modification *but* continuation'—the two being opposed to one another; and 'modification *from which results* continuation', the latter proceeding from the former. Indeed, to think about transition implies conceiving at the same time of the inseparability of the two: that the modification breaks with the continuation, as being its contrary, but at the same time does not cease to promote the latter as it emerges from the wasting away which threatens it. Because it is only through the modification that the continuation remains active and endures—since the point of view developed in China was not really of essence and identification but of energy invested in the process of things. In this way there might be continuous 'communication' (the connected meaning of *tong*) between modification and continuation, and the process under way might not become exhausted.

Let us not look for a further example. Let us just consider what I am simply doing: writing. What, properly speaking, is a literary transition, or how one passes from one sentence to the next, from one paragraph to the next, from one chapter to the next? Does this not mean breaking both with what has come before while pursuing a thought through this rupture which is prolonged in order that it can develop? The blank space left at the heart of the text is not empty but on the contrary is the fertile place within which, without one having written, some text continues to advance; where some flagging thought finds, by discontinuing, the force of its continuity: where the argument, giving way to lack, is called upon to link itself together. On this subject one will verify the formula of antiquity in *The Book of Changes*: 'exhaustion from which modification, modification from which continuation, continuation from which duration' (an example will be found in the literary realm in *Wenxin diaolong*, Chapter 29, 'Tong-bian'). Or one will revisit in one's mind this beautiful image taken from in the *Literary Arts* of ancient China: when one is in a boat and raises the oars for a moment, such is the art of transition. One no longer paddles, the movement of rowing—of writing—is interrupted, but the boat is carried along and pursues its course.

Notes

1 The references by Jullien to *The Book of Changes*, the *Yi Jing* or *I Ching*, do not appear to correspond with the English translations. See note in Bibliography.—Trans.

Chapter 3

THE SNOW MELTS

(OR HOW THE BIAS OF BEING PREVENTS US
FROM THINKING ABOUT THE TRANSITION)

It would be wrong, I think, to consider the diversity of cultures from the perspective of difference. This is because *difference* relates to identity as well as its opposite and, as a result, to the demand for identity—we can see well enough how many false debates are pursued today. To consider the diversity of cultures on the basis of their differences leads to their being attributed with specific features and it encloses each of them within a unity of principle. The risks this brings are immediately apparent. We know that every culture is plural, as much as it is singular, and that it is ceaselessly mutating; that it is led to homogenize itself at the same time as it is to heterogenize itself, divesting its identity as well as re-identifying itself, that it conforms but also resists; imposes itself as the dominant culture while, at the same time, provoking dissent against it. Official and *underground*: the cultural is always being unfolded and moving faster, but only between these two movements.

This is why I have preferred, in the course of my open work-in-progress between China and Europe, to deal with *divergences* rather than differences. Because divergence (*écart*) promotes a point of view which is no longer that of identification, in favour of what I will call exploration: it envisages the extent to which various possibilities can be deployed and what intersections are discernable in thought. At the same time, it brings to the fore the preliminary question that has not been developed within philosophy itself, which is, *to what extent*, in China or in Greece, on one front or another, dealing with them in one way or another, can the frontiers of what is thinkable be discerned and, more than this, can an inkling of what one has not thought to think be ventured? This is because the slightest perceived divergence (*écart*) between cultures, which can be worked upon, however prospectively, opens the compasses more widely, or unfolds the fan. It causes a lack to appear, digs a corner into what is unsuspected, that of the *prerequisite* of thought (pre-notional, pre-categorized, pre-questioned...), that is all the more resistant because it lurks further upstream from the well-known 'pre-judgements' or prejudices with which philosophy may be incriminated—how then to take a step back within its spirit?

Therefore, instead of ending in a tidying-up operation, within a framework with pre-established parameters and executed side by side, which is where difference leads, *divergence* (*écart*) allows another perspective to emerge, it loosens, or exposes, a fresh enticing possibility (an adventure). Once again, I mention this here to respond to an objection which I am amazed still to be accused of: if I am attentive to such divergences, to the slightest divergence (*écart*), this is not so as to isolate cultures from one another and enclose them in their own worlds (my whole work consists on the contrary of bringing them into dialogue), but to detach thought from what, on both sides, it assumes to be 'evidence', from one or other source, and about which it does not even have an idea, and to procure it some angles from which it can break with the stand-off and reactivate itself. This is where divergence (*écart*) becomes a tool. Because instead of baldly assuming some unity or specificity of principle, on each side, one which we might know beforehand (although where did this projection come to us from?), divergence (*écart*) sets what it has separated in tension and *discovers one through the other*, reflects one in the other. It also advantageously displaces the viewing perspective, not only shifting that of distinction, characteristic of difference, to one of *distance* and, as a result, of the open field within thought; but also, consequently, from the question of identity to the hope of a *fertility*. It enables consideration of the diversity of cultures or thought as so many available *resources*, of which any intelligence can make good use in order to enlarge and reacquaint itself, and from which benefit may be gained, which means that they would not be lost, which is the risk run by contemporary uniformity as a result of globalization (see Jullien 2008: 219).

I am not wondering what it is that 'properly' characterizes Greek or Chinese culture and thought according to some native originality: one is wary of too much that is arbitrary in essentialist representations of culture, fossilized as they moreover are by tradition. I am rather concerned to ask which resources they have each deployed and promoted, in their inventiveness, and which can be put to good use by our common intelligence today. But suddenly this appears to me already achieved. The fact that Greek thought might be articulated in the language of Being has allowed it to deploy the requirement of *determination—logos—*allowing it to abstract and produce 'truth' and, as a result, to construct this very requirement indefinitely in thought, the very requirement of which science and philosophy has been able to take advantage. But at the same time it has deprived itself of an inverse, concealed or abandoned fertility, which might allow the indeterminable to be grasped from the passage or transition. This is why *transition* is really—'logically', i.e. from the point of view of *logos*—the sticking point of Greek thought. It contains what appears symptomatic of the handicap from which Greek thought suffers; that which it is less inclined, because less well equipped, to think in broad terms, so that consequently we in Europe have paid less attention to it. It is a 'handicap' that of course I can measure only by a comparison and through a divergence (*écart*): in this case, in relation to the other possibility I have just begun to outline and that has been greatly utilized by Chinese thought in a way that is foreign to that of the Greeks. Indeed, as it has followed other paths opened up by language, Chinese thought has been able in contrast to go beyond the lack of demarcation of the transition, and thus also of the silent transformation which results from it, the perspective from which to approach any process of existence. Are life and the world not in *continuous transition?* This is something very different from the 'mobility' invoked in philosophy.

It will therefore not be a question here, as I circulate between these systems of thought that have been foreign to one another, of *baldly* 'comparing', by giving labels to both of them, whether in terms of resemblances or differences, but of investigating their respective richness, like a diviner, testing the coherences, as they are dipped into here and there, enabling us to think what for us has been unthought. We can imagine that this can be attained only through indirect means, by driving it out, through divergence (*écart*), since it can only be grasped obliquely (if not we would have thought it . . .). Thus, the bias of Being calls upon the determination which is recapitulated in the maxim that has for such a long time guided the work of thought behind the scenes in Europe to the extent that it has passed unperceived through it. Let me formulate it: the more something is *determined*, the more it 'exists'. Or, as Hegel said in the opposite sense 'pure Being', when it is still undetermined, is not yet *distinguished* in any way from 'pure nothingness': it is only a 'complete emptiness', and there is 'within it *nothing* with which to see', and in truth I have not yet, as I name it, said anything (1969: 82). Moreover, in this respect, can we not see the European painter of the classical age as the active brother and accomplice of the philosopher? This is because he paints feature by feature, with tenacity, all the time towards greater determination and so as to create more 'being'. That shimmering dress trimmed with lace or that hand placed upon it, in which the slightest vein can be perceived, the slightest flaw discerned: how far can one succeed in creating 'being' through the precision and distinction brought to it? On the other hand, what revolution has been needed in the modern age to valorize what was not painted and advocate the outline?

That the transition would, par excellence, be *indeterminable*, as we have already measured in terms of the difficulties encountered by Plato and Aristotle, is therefore to be treated in the proper and rigorous sense: it is what no longer has a limit or mark of possible separation allowing one thing to be distinguished from another—the black from the white, or the low note from the high. Whether it is a question of grey or of the median note, the transition abrogates the frontier within them and consequently draws them away from the mastery of Being and its power. While the *logos* is 'definition', *horismos*, all of the Greeks tell us, it carves out the limits between genus and characteristics that allow us to recognize the Being in it, transition is par excellence that which holds us back from being able to say how far any one characteristic or quality extends, where the other begins. It withdraws the pertinence from both and reabsorbs them. Consequently, it undoes those portions which Being allocates to itself.

The transition in fact *undoes*. Would it be worthwhile to measure the extent to which it does this? Because all by itself it undoes—or deconstructs—our old philosophical tools. It undoes nothing less than the 'idea' as a universal form, that of the intelligible, since it is 'within the self as self-assurance', says Plato, in full possession of its self and arising only from its self, admitting in it and, on principle, that there is nothing other than such a 'self', *auto*, which must therefore remain 'pure' and intransigent in respect of all mixing. This is the operation of 'distinguishing' from which comes its essence (*diairesis tôn eidôn*). Or if it is, inversely, within the individual that the essence is sought, in other words in its 'substance' (*ousia*), within which, according to Aristotle, all research into being as being is directed, the transition still unmakes it: since this essence is itself obtained only by passing 'from difference to difference', and going to the point of 'ultimate' difference—as being to the exclusion of anything other, having one *or* another quality (1984b, Chapters 12–15; see also, before him, Plato 1961c, 208d). The definition, by which Being is differentiated, always proceeds from a power to isolate.

Let's go into the heart of the tangible and the same thing is found again. Because not only are contrary ideas excluded, as Plato tells us, but so is everything which is concrete and which essentially contributes to one or the other by right of ownership. So snow has cold as its property and it cannot then coexist in any way with heat (Plato 1961b, 102–3). Now what is it about snow when it melts? Plato, we note, is not able to think of the snow *in the process of melting*—as it becomes water. The phrase is again confusing, because it gets entangled in Being: 'snow, being what it is, can never admit heat and still remain snow, just as it was before, only now with the addition of heat.... Again, fire must either withdraw or cease to exist at the approach of cold' (1961b 103: 85). Plato (should we be surprised?) has once again missed the phenomenon of the transition. Or rather that moment of transition, where the one hastens to relinquish its place to the other, even for so short a moment, a 'sudden', a pure intervening period that is without extension and therefore without existence. Could this give us a good reason to pass over it in silence? But we still notice it when we look out of the window: hardly has it fallen, or even as it is in process of falling, even when it is still swirling about, do we not so often see the snow imperceptibly (but interminably, one might say) in the process of melting before our eyes?

Do we find in Chinese thought anything that by comparison, by means of its divergence (*écart*), opens a way out for us? Not expressing itself in the language of Being, Chinese thought is by contrast at ease in taking account of the state of 'what one sees but does not perceive', or of 'what one listens to but does not hear': that state where the perceptible breaks up and loses its specificity, disqualifies itself, 'loses its taste', without for all that lapsing into the invisible of metaphysics; where the demarcations are undone and which, through its indifferentiation, allows the incessant transition of things to appear (Lao-tzu 1992, § 14: 16). It is even such a state, preceding delimitations-definitions, whose continuity 'cannot be named' but whose indistinction again leads us beneficently towards the fundamental harmony which Taoists have called the *Tao*, in which 'the configuration is without configuration', as is said in the *Tao te Ching*, or in which the phenomenon is without a characteristic materiality which could individualize it (*wu wu zhi xiang*). Every delimiting feature is withdrawn from it: the *tao* (the way), if it must at any price be defined, is essentially *transition*, and this is why it is indefinable (and not for some 'mystical' reason, as we prefer to think in the West). But it is also why, instead of intruding into the terms of Being, the only thing that can be said—a formula immediately hushing any ontological inquisition—'Profoundly still, it seems to be there' (*si huo cun*) (ibid., § 4: 10).

It is time, in opening the compasses so wide, for us to measure its consequences. Passing from the *ontological* to the *taoique*, we no longer find it difficult to recognize, against the need for a determination of *logos*, the legitimacy of the 'vague' and 'hazy' nature of the process of things (*hu-huang*). How better to express the median *indifferentiation* which characterizes it than by this double retreat from the limit on each side, both beforehand and afterwards: 'When you face it you do not see its head/when you follow it you do not see its back'? (ibid., § 14: 16). How better to characterize the suspension in this respect than by these images: 'Their weariness was that of one crossing a river in winter,/their caution was that of one in fear of all around'? (ibid., § 17: 17). The image belongs to the *tao*, by this fact, the least image-making; instead of characterizing, everything that may characterize is removed; even as it keeps us at the heart of the phenomenal and the perceptible, it leads us to the brink of their effacement: where it is non-flavour that is enjoyed (the 'blandness'). Thus it says best what Greek philosophy did not grant: 'dissolving like ice on the point of melting', says the *tao* of Lao-tzu, subsequently. As though he was responding to Plato and literally taking the opposite tack.

In this respect another divergence (*écart*) intervenes, conjoined, which bears upon the status of 'what' is changed in the transition. At least I can myself only begin to express it in substantivizing Greek terms: *ti*, 'some thing' or 'what'. Is there always a 'what' (change)? Because everything which changes does so between contrary terms (*antikeimena*), as Aristotle says in summarizing and conciliating all his precursors at the beginning of his *Physics* (1984a 189–90: 223–4). And, in the same way, the Chinese generically call the opposites between which the change has taken place *yin* and *yang*. But Aristotle is not satisfied with this: it is necessary to introduce a third term in addition to these contraries, which is again an ontologizing term—in addition to or rather placed 'underneath' them: this is the 'substratum' (*hupokeimenon*), which is the 'sub-ject' of (or to) the change). Not only are opposites, like those of heat and cold, considered to be 'elements' or 'principles', but so too is *what* happens between them: like the snow which from being colder becomes warmer, 'in which' these opposites replace each other.

From this point we can no longer extricate ourselves from this question: When the snow is in the process of melting 'is' it still snow? Is it not already water? Let us decompose the question: What is the *thing* that exists (or does it still exist?) in the state of transition that is 'sustained' between the two (and of which Aristotle therefore makes his costly 'hypo-thesis')? In other words, by maintaining this fictional unity of a *third term*, one which, in addition to the two categories, would be affected by the change between the two contraries, does not this thought of the substrate-subject stand in the way of grasping the transition while projecting and extending its identity even through the transformation? This question may appear purely speculative but it is not, because it goes right to the heart of the 'subjects' that we are. Because transition, like that of ice becoming water, is precisely the state in which, between dis-identification and re-identification, the question of *identity* can no longer still be 'sup-posed'. To make such an assumption from the start prevents us from giving a place to the transition and recognizing it.

For its part, Chinese thought avoids this difficulty for the simple reason that it does not conceive of having to suggest a *third term*, a substrate-subject, for the change. Here we can even locate precisely where the divergence (*écart*) appears and how Chinese thought, at this point separating with the Greek, opens at the same time another possibility. Since it does not approach reality in terms of 'Being' and therefore of 'substance' which, as such, cannot contain contraries, because they would be irreconcilable with it, in Chinese thought these oppositions alone are sufficient to account for the coherence of all change. Aristotle had actually envisaged this possibility, which he then immediately refused as plainly illogical. So let us try to enter further into this thought, like the Chinese, in which everything proceeds from a play of polarities (*yin* and *yang*)—let us give it its chance: where the 'deployment' of the one necessarily responds to the 'contraction' of the other, but also where the one spills into the other and cannot renew itself except through this other. The necessity for a 'substance' then disappears and the idea of 'what' might be maintained within the change becomes incongruous. The very idea of 'identity' is taken apart. So, from the outset it was the idea of identity that silent transformations came up against, engendering an irrepressible feeling of strangeness. Coming face to face with the photograph of twenty years earlier (do not photographs on identity documents have to be periodically renewed?), or a friend whom one bumps into again after many years: it cannot be 'him'; yet at the same time as it cannot be other than him and so on.

To what point can we avoid being drawn into the anxiety I have started to reveal about an analysis of change? From the—'hypo-thetical'—substrate-subject of the transformation, it is here transferred into language. In fact, the way language is conceived handicaps all the more what can be thought about the transition, because at the same time it organizes (although this is also the source of its power of determination) the word in *predication*. This necessary substrate of change is the no-less-necessary subject of the sentence in support of description. As Aristotle constructed it, from the *Physics* to the *Metaphysics* (1984b, Chapter 3), this substrate-subject is, as the subject of the proposition, what allows everything else to be expressed 'categorically' by way of attribute, i.e. according to categories, but which itself is expressed as nothing else. Should we again ask whether this predicative subject is adequate to account for the transition? I would say no, for at least two reasons. First, because having become undone in the course of the transition, this purely assignative structure according to which, for the subject existing in itself, it would end up *additionally* being one thing or another: snow does not additionally, by virtue of attribution or supplementary description, soften or exist in the process of melting. On the other hand, the predicative statement separates various qualities, adding some to others but expressing all of them independently of the transformation, while they remain inseparable in the transition and make the unbreakable 'whole' of the transformation, moreover rendering it imperceptible since nothing is differentiated: there is no snow which becomes translucent *and* also becomes soft *and* also becomes warm, etc.

In contrast we can see that, on the Chinese side, the enunciative plan of the *Tao te Ching* is entirely conceived to thwart such a predicative world—for this reason it is inventive and resists translation into our languages: as soon as it is rendered it into a European language, the sentence has to be made predicative and the *tao* has to be essentialized again (thus giving it a mystical interpretation, by attributing a hypostatization to it, as Westerners inevitably do of the Tao of Taoism). Otherwise, the *Tao te Ching* recognizes that if 'forced' expression there is, it is to be decanted from one term to the other so that each of the terms which follow us prevents it from remaining in the specification of any of them and being envisaged apart, by rights, from a qualifying point of view: 'Imposing on it a name, I call it great./Greatness means it goes;/going means reaching afar;/reaching afar means return . . .' (Lao-tzu, 1992, §15 and § 25: 17 and 24). Each of these terms does not ostensibly serve here as a 'termination', defining and apprehending meaning, but as a bridge. Hardly has it been expressed than it is withdrawn; hardly has a meaning been sketched out than it is modified; indeed, the meaning is constituted only to be taken apart. It *un*-determines, just as the image then unmakes images. Neither is there any extant subject—not even the *tao*, or rather it is re-absorbed by the *tao*—to which one or other quantity would be successively attributable; but each appellation is transferred as it is advanced and transformed into what follows: the sentence itself is its transition.

In producing these equivalences, the *Tao te Ching* equally openly eludes the ultimate methodological consequence of the bias of Being as developed by the Greeks: the principle of non-contradiction. This does not bother the *Tao te Ching*. The principle of non-contradiction really expresses the opposite, in the form of prohibition, which becomes the ontological requirement par excellence: that the same thing cannot, at the same time and from the same perspective, be said to be both this and not this. As such, it renders the transition illogical: that the thing would at the same time still be this and already not-this. But is the ice or snow in the process of melting not 'at the same time' (*ama*) still firm and already its opposite, at the same time soft and not soft, melted and not melted? Thus we can see that Plato and Aristotle, the very people who formalized this principle for all future generations, had problems in dealing with the transition whenever they could not avoid referring to it: it upsets this system of exclusive determinations and their words straightaway become confused. It becomes what a commentator would call an obscure passage, a part of the text that is uncertain, an error of the copyist... As though this was not the symptom of a disability impossible to mask.

Chapter 4

DO MODIFICATIONS HAVE A BEGINNING?

Looking afresh at the ancient case of 'motion', Bergson warns us that, ordinarily, we 'view' change but we 'do not perceive it' (1984: 1366). We do not perceive it because our intelligence separates, isolates and stabilizes. Let us try to re-educate it, because, to recover the living perception of change, it would first of all be necessary to represent all change and movement as indivisible. Yet we apprehend both movement and change by decomposing them into successive positions and we allow the passage by which the interval is crossed to elude us. If we are really compelled, mentally, to introduce the need for a passage, we recoil indefinitely from the moment of envisaging it. This is why we are always, through bad habits, reduced here to assuming a substratum-support for change of which metaphysics cannot rid itself; we always assume *beneath* this change 'things' which change and therefore lose, because they are divided, tightened and as if weighed down by them, the essential continuity of this 'shifting' that is life.

But I wonder whether what Bergson describes here as a failing of the intelligence is not actually the result of the language in which he thinks. In other words, would not the idea that 'things' lie 'beneath' change rather be imputable to the great European language? Thus any perceived divergence (*écart*), allowing us to stand back from it, will already (however slightly) shift this triangle by means of which the Greeks took a considerable option on thought which I have just summarized according to three conjoined biases: determination, substantivization (substantialization) and predication. In the first place, that the ideal of *logos*, as Aristotle recommends, would be to eliminate indetermination and ambiguity so as to render thought as 'clear' as it can possibly be, and first of all thanks to multiple operations of distinction, morphological and syntaxical even before being semantic, that European language is steered towards effecting (1). Then, that not only would the nominal need to be separated from the verbal from the outset (according to the primary distinction of the Greek language: *rémata/onomata*), but that it should moreover be understood as referring to an actual being, 'holding itself within', both substantive and substance, serving as support for Being as much as for the proposition (2). Finally and consequently that the function of this proposition might be to predicate, i.e. to assign to this sub-ject forming basis, in a more or less casual way (the 'accident' Aristotle speaks of), that which from this point can do no more than attribute properties or qualities to itself, and distribute side by side, like so many possible states (3). Under the pressure of these concurrent constraints the phenomenon of the transition 'logically' eludes us. But can the grip of this vice be released?

It is true that Plato once audaciously risked 'extracting' Being from all sides in order temporarily to take care of the opposing cases of motions (*Theaetetus*, 1961d, 157b: 861). He throws down this challenge: let's cease to speak of either 'something' or 'of something', neither 'of me' nor of 'this' or 'that', nor to use any other name so it would 'determine' something. But let's just say, articulating 'according to nature': 'becoming and acting and disappearing and altering' (*gignomena, poioumena, apollumena, alloioumena*). Since it is true that, as Plato recognized, as soon as something is determined by *logos*, no matter how slightly, it is easy to be confused. However, one is obliged to admit: even in this sentence in which he tries most to put aside the conditions of Greek language, without any naming of subject, even indefinitely, to which might be ascribed successively this 'becoming—making—disappearing—altering', Plato no less implies, in the form of these participles present in the plural neutral and according to the object, a nominal referent to which they refer grammatically and that they describe. Even if the latter is ostensibly removed from the sentence. Consequently, this is an exceptional breakthrough, a Platonic release which lasts as long as a few words, ironical and inspired, as one might attempt a heroic breakthrough against an adversary: in it, finally, the idiomatic expression of language can be seen challenged, hidden away as it is on all sides and holding our word in its traps. But barely outlined as it is, how could the enterprise not come to a sudden end? Immediately? Because the Greek cannot escape from the articulation of 'beings', either from declension or from attribution, neither from gender nor from number, and even coordinated as they are, these phenomenalist qualifications remain propped up against Being and leave the gap between them untouched...

Nevertheless, we would not dream of stopping at the formulae which express in Chinese how, from what is only a 'full stop' or an 'end point', the implied process of transformation extends from one phase (one phrase) to another to the point of including them all and then slackening off. Insofar as these formulae seem obvious as they are reeled off homologically one after the other, so much do they flow expectedly in the Chinese language, offering little asperity to which our attention could hold (*Zhongyong*, § 24; see Jullien 2006: 144). So the terms of this sequence could indifferently be considered to be nominals— verbs—adjectives, and there is no preliminary indication of 'what' this sentence is about: can I myself render it in a way at all intelligible in French without immediately re-integrating our substantivist and predicative grammar into it? In trying to negotiate between these exigencies as best I can, I would translate it as: 'effectively introduced and so actualized' (either to actualize or actualization),

actualized and so manifest,
manifest and so illuminating,
illuminating and so sets/setting in motion
setting in motion and so modification
modification and so transformation

(*Zhongyong*, § 24)

As there is no sup-position here whatsoever about what would be said in this enunciation, that no 'thing' is therefore placed here 'within' the change, only the functions which link up are evoked: as no sub-ject is expressed or even suggested, only a continuous effectiveness is described as being deployed through these successive modalities. But what is understood by effectiveness? Unassigned as it is, effectiveness appears precisely to be that which defeats all transcendence of a subject governing action as well as proposition, rendering it artificial. As it is here neither declined nor conjugated, neither predicated nor referred, as it is not sharply distinguished between the passive and the active, the syntaxical alone (*ze*) expresses the *induction*. From the local to the global (*yi qu/tian xia*), an influence is objectivized, takes consistency, is deployed, illuminates, and is finally prescribed. Even the passage to movement (*dong*) is no longer, as it was in Plato, the object of a rupture, but proceeds from the earlier 'illumination'. Thus we verify it even in morality: when, from simply being 'manifest', it becomes luminous and illuminates, the exemplary nature of the Sage alone weakens the others ('sets them in motion') and prompts them.

But can the progression of the transition still be read where the expected caesura is at its most glaring and we are dealing not simply with the movement from immobility to mobility but from 'non-being' to 'being', as the Greeks would have understood it, or at least between the arrival of life and what has preceded it? Again when translating it will be necessary to retain as much as possible of the Chinese idiom, here taken from the *Chuang tzu*, under our linguistic constraints and constructing it: 'mingled-indistinct-between', the Chinese text literally says: when modified (modification), there is breath; when modified-breath, there is actualization; when modified-actualizing, there is life' (Guo Qingfan 1983: 615). The French translator renders this formulation like this, rearranging the syntax of the sentence, as though it did not happen there, and so giving it a completely different meaning: 'something fleeting and ungraspable is transformed into breath, breath into form and form into life' (Tchouang-tse 1973: 145). The meaning is not incorrect, properly speaking (the translation is even impeccable), but through its French construction it organizes what we expect in a quite different way. From the outset a substrate-subject, even the most indefinite possible, a 'something', has been incorporated and this is restyled predicatively ('fleeting and ungraspable'). Thereby from the outset the translation forces into our language a question which is not justified by anything in the Chinese, which is rendered without an object: therefore, from where does this 'something', as fleeing as it may be, come, and is there not an inevitable cut (but why and how?) due to its springing up? Or has this been effected *ex nihilo*, etc.? And consequently is not God necessary as justification for its Creation? And so on. From a divergence (*écart*) of language unfolds a completely different way of being able to conceive of life and of articulating its destiny. All philosophy, no matter how radical its questioning, comes only afterwards, and it is enfolded in the idiom which it can only reflect.

For how could the philosopher by his own efforts escape from what he finds 'enfolded' within the language (as the French familiarly say: 'fold it up and it's tidy') and to which, without considering the determinism it impresses on his thought, he is nevertheless predisposed? The most intriguing thing, when we pass from Europe to China, is that the questions that we are posing are ones we could not fail to pose when we pass over to the other side, in other words when we slip into the other language where they are no longer posed, *no longer* have to be posed: not because they have been resolved in it, but because they have dissolved. Also, in the *Tao te Ching*, the caesura which is apparent in the European phrase (from 'non-being' to 'being') is absorbed, since birth itself is part of a continuation (*Lao tze*, § 15): just as if, when we see the troubled waters, we let them rest, they will gradually become clear and limpid, so '[what is] at rest (if it is placed for a long time in movement) will gradually dawn' (or 'grows' or 'lives': *sheng*). No longer causing a rupture, the origin of life is no longer an enigma. It is not even a question—*the* question—any more because it is found to be integrated, discreetly implicated, into the course of the transition.

Is there always, therefore, a beginning to modifications, even to those that are most marked? It would be nice to think that this beginning might remain blurred when passing from the invisible to the visible, and even that there would not be an easily discovered beginning, since it plunges into the indistinction of what is embryonic at the heart of which one could again go back indefinitely. But could it be the same at the heart of the visible, when one looks at it from both sides and the objects are juxtaposed before our eyes? Would there not always be, as the blurring disperses, a boundary between them? Has there not always been a demarcation line according to which the sea is separated from the beach, a decisive point, a break in the scene, where the footpath begins to ascend? But already we notice that as each wave comes it never deposits its line of spume on the bank at exactly the same place: it leaves an uncertain fringe to the transition from one element to another, from the ground to the water. This is all the more so when it comes to the landscape. When we follow the Rhone along a straight line from the Mediterranean, or even along any path rising through the passes, where (or when?) does the South of France become the North? Where is the separation to be found? We nevertheless leave behind us other skies, other odours, a distinctness in the silhouette of the land and the form of things—but where does this bath of light come to an end and its revocation begin? Because it is not olive trees or cicadas which make up the South ... Neither is it the warmth embedded in the stones or the roofs of the houses. There is not a substrate-thing— the possible 'subject' of a discourse—which 'should be' the South. The transformation is rather, one of *ambiance*, too global to be grasped in a predicative fashion and quantitatively; and the transition continues for too long for it to be marked on a map.

When I travel from Paris to Brittany, I often look out of the window of the train as I come closer to the great modification I anticipate. But it always eludes me. At Le Mans we are still in the dependency of Paris and the legendary 'basin' where the landscape remains open. But at Laval we have definitively slipped into a strange, remote land, one that has become secret, in spite of its flatness. And yet there is no demarcation between the two. Is the mutation read in the passage, in the subsoil, from limestone to granite, or from the tiles to the slate on the roofs of the houses, or in the greenness of the meadows, or in the form of the bells or even in the skies, no longer tenderly 'veiled in pink vapours' (Baudelaire), but where the clouds are from that point on structured in dizzying forms, so sharply chiselled by the setting sun? When therefore has the marine element started to appear in the atmosphere or in the life of people? One thing is certain: even if nothing indicates it in the relief, everything has changed before our eyes, without its being perceived, and even to the way the sun sets behind the clouds. A great shattering has occurred in the course of the journey without there being a crack to betray it. It is as if nothing has happened. Because this expectancy, or this ambiance, this 'atmosphere', are not demarcated in terms of properties and are therefore impervious to our ontological engagement.

This is also why all descriptive poetry remains boring, despite the genius of the poets: because it always assumes 'things', forming a base whose aspect should be determined, whose properties should be described. The sea 'is grey', the sky 'is dark' . . . Each time we speak of a 'thing', enfolded into its attributes, when we would like to evoke a landscape ; we find we are confined to a stubborn assignation, whereas what we would like to capture is a *pervasive* nature, communicating everywhere without limit. How many obstinately risked infractions and diversions have been necessary, under the impulse of the poetic (even if this is only the legendary 'poetic licence' won in the face of grammar), for us finally to undermine this attachment to the predicative function culminating all-too advantageously in France in romantic abundance, so as not to break ourselves upon it . . . and for Baudelaire insidiously to turn away from this impracticable but so-long-trodden path?

Chapter 5

TRANSITION OR CROSSING—
AGEING HAS ALWAYS ALREADY STARTED

There is something else which caused the Greeks to misunderstand the phenomenon of the transition and it is related more to their physics than to their ontology. Approaching nature, *phusis*, in terms not, as the Chinese have done, through correlated factors, that is *yin* and *yang*, but of the body in movement, they conceived change to be like movement, although it might be treated as appropriate for the genus while movement only relates to the species; this assimilation can be seen to pass from one to the other, from change to movement (*metabolé-kinesis*), so as to endure throughout the whole history of Western philosophy, finding itself still intact in Bergson who, we nevertheless know, was very cautious about the misrepresentation of change by borrowing from space. Does this therefore imply that change is decisively, and even irreparably, conceived on the model of movement? First of all we know that change might be envisaged, like movement, from those edges or extremities that are its points of departure and arrival, just as the moving body gets from point A to point B. 'Since all change goes from something to something' (*ek tinos—eis ti*), says Aristotle after just having considered the colour grey or the median point as oppositions (1984a: 380).

Is this assimilation of change to movement auspicious? Is it because all change must be understood as going *from* somewhere *to* somewhere else? In other words, must it only be envisaged from its beginning and its end, which form its extremities and give consistency to what lies between them only through their divergence (*écart*) alone, in a way that is consequently *distensional* and no longer treated as *transitional*, as circulation and continuity? (see Jullien 2001, Chapter 3, 'Distension-transition'). Such an option is decisive, in fact, because, at a stroke and without our paying attention to it, it above all causes a shattering in the way in which we envisage life, digging out this alternative beneath it: is life *transition*, in which each moment is uncovered and counts in its own right, and is pregnant with the next? Or is it a *crossing*, so that what counts beforehand is the arrival? In the latter case, it is charged with enigma: it is no longer life, properly speaking, but becomes 'existence'. Its course being engendered from within itself, and as such being integrated with the natural, it immediately subsides into a fathomless question, one from which metaphysics and religion draw their strength. It means that it will no longer be possible to avoid questioning oneself about the destination of this journey (a privileged metaphor for such a 'running ahead', *Vorlaufen*, as Heidegger calls it). When will we arrive at the 'port' (death) that is its expected end?

This is a destination which it is so much more important to specify, even for Aristotle, although he is undoubtedly the least tormented of all of our philosophers, since the Greeks have burdened it with all expectation of the end, *telos*, which is at once the aim and conclusion. Because all movement is understood in relation to the end ('entelechy') of what is in power within it, Aristotle tells us in what has remained a famous definition (1984a). It is the same thing for change. Aristotle is just as unable to understand anything about ageing. Because how would it be the conclusion and end of what had previously been 'in power' within it, just as a constructed house, which he offers us as an example, is one with the operation of constructing it? Aristotle is just as attached to all those 'movements' enumerated as a result, arranged under the same model of 'accomplishment' and as though equivalents: 'Similarly with learning, doctoring, rolling, jumping, ripening, ageing,' he says (ibid.: 225a: 342).

I have lingered over Aristotle's enumeration here because it shows very well how *ageing*, caught between the two logics, of finality on the one hand and distension on the other, instead of transition, becomes literally illegible. On a larger scale, can not the same thing be said about what is more generally called 'life'? Because neither is ageing arranged in relation to the perspective of an aim and a conclusion of what is aimed at (like learning or doctoring, according to Aristotle's list, or even, if necessary, growth), nor is it included between the beginning and end of a change-movement (as is a jump or ripening). Indeed, just like snow in the process of melting, growing old only summarizes all the obstacle points of Greek thought. First, to age is not what would happen in addition to what I would be as a 'subject', but is inseparable from whatever it is that is my 'essence', my *ousia*: to grow old is not one possible attribute among many that can be detached from others, and cannot therefore be understood in predicative way. On the other hand, we know that growing old does not result in the decomposition of features or qualities separately from one another but as coupled together, and whose totality constitutes the ageing: I can review as many of the various aspects as I want (the eyes, the complexion, the skin, the sight . . .), but no matter how long the inventory may be, it will still be unable to identify anything (or only superficially) about the transition which is in operation.

Ageing is therefore neither attributive nor distributive, neither distinctive nor additive. Equally, to age undoes the very foundations of the condition of possibility of all identity, and this is really what the Narrator inevitably has to recognize, as so many others have done, when the last morning at the home of the Princess de Guermantes comes and the 'metamorphosis was so complete, their identity so impossible to establish—that old monk, for instance, in a corner of the room and the notorious rake whom one remembered, were they the same person?' (Proust 1981b: 319). Ageing equally unravels the principle of non-contradiction, since this is also simply the logical reversal of what the principle of identity names in a positive way: not only because of 'the appearance of this old woman', as Proust noted a little earlier 'the juxtaposition of the two appearances, the young and the old, seems so totally to exclude the possibility of their belonging to the same person' (ibid.: 312); but especially because to grow old is at the same time and from the same perspective, indissolubly, still to be young and yet already old: old because wear and tear and death are soon at work within us; and young, because life is renewed with an amazing obstinacy, that the heart still beats with vigour and one still gets up in the freshness, and even as though it were the first ever, of yet another morning.

To this can presently be added, adulterating the *ageing*, what Greek physics prescribes for us as the beginning and end of movement, points of departure and arrival. On the one hand, does ageing have a beginning? When 'and from where' did I start to age? No beginning is assignable to it: no matter how far back one goes, one has always started to get old. Cells are already dying as the foetus is being modelled. The ageing has always already started. On the other hand, towards what form-end does ageing extend (according to that great Greek coupling, *eidos-telos*), just as to cure tends 'through entelechy' towards a cure or building to construction? The Greek misunderstanding in this respect is to have confounded that which is of the order of the goal with that which is of the order of the result; or rather, more insidiously, of having located the logic of consequences under the hypertrophied logic of finality: that of the process under the model of action and its aim. Or again, to have considered all success as a destination. Because to age, we must repeat, 'tends' towards nothing, but we can gradually measure its effects.

Because European philosophy has privileged finality, has been preoccupied as a priority with the 'towards what' (*eis ti*) and with the destination, concentrating on the result and not on the transition, it has stepped over old age. Has it even noticed it? It has passed over it in silence and kept only the End in sight: that is, Death. Heidegger again—thought of the 'towards' and the destination, of the *wozu* and the *Zukunft*: would mankind not be defined existentially as 'being towards death'? (Jullien 2001, Chapter 6). And so the consequence is this statement:

European philosophy has developed without discontinuing a philosophy of death—without disarming it, one must acknowledge, and through a heroism of thought—erecting death as an explosive event, one that breaks everything and judges everything. Cutting everything; crying out when its hour has come, indeed sounding the bugle like its trumpets . . . But we do not find, anywhere in Europe, a philosophy of silent ageing and its discreet eroding. Only, here and there, some advice and consolation calling for serenity through resignation: *De senectute*.

Nevertheless, would not this constant and silent passage which constitutes 'ageing', as undeniable as it is, teach us more about life itself; does it not already definitively let us glimpse what is effective, so widespread and discreet is it that it is ordinarily imperceptible, about all we project and busily construct about the End? But European philosophy has no less placed death as a gleam on the horizon as a culminating, fascinating and apocalyptic point, *towards* which everything converges and will be suddenly resolved: the place where, tearing aside the veil, the anticipated Truth is finally to be revealed. Because this paroxysmal point in the ideological montage of the West is, very conveniently, both at the same time the place where the ontological alternative par excellence is radicalized and dramatized (and made absolute), captivating desire to the point of vertigo: *to be or not to be (esti e ouk esti*, as

Parmenides had already said); and where at once the suspense and its resolution is dramatized: between Loss and Salvation, between the mystery and the absurd.

If philosophy had transferred its attention to the transition of ageing, as something which we are nevertheless faced with everywhere and which has always already started, it would undoubtedly have refrained from making of death a point of scrutiny which definitively cuts off everything, an invitation, in a great game of double or nothing, to the wager of Faith or rather to the tragic hardening. It would have approached death as the ultimate result—the avatar—of ageing that begins so soon, no longer as a Rupture and leap into the Indescribable, but in the dependency and continuation of ageing. Consequently, it would no longer be questioning it from the point of view of a Meaning: death would not be more absurd if it led to mystery. But it is *outside-meaning*. It would cease to be an enigma and become an epilogue. Moreover, what radical questioning would not already entail no longer speaking in this way of 'death' (Death as detachable, raised up, personified), but in terms of a process, as 'dying' (as we speak of 'ageing'), as the Chinese—not being able to distinguish morphologically between the verb and the substantive—are obliged to do? Better still: does it not, in effacing the rupture, usually name death itself as a 'transformation' (*hua*)?

In fact, if death was approached as the individual and momentary outcome of the silent transformations we see taking place everywhere, the truth would then be left tacitly harnessed—already, in a discreet way, as the days go by, just as the transition itself continues, without consequently 'loosening' and resolving the fateful question. Indeed, would the question still need to be constructed, at a distance, provoking contradictory hypotheses and endlessly giving rise to these debates, like those between naturalism and religion or idealism and materialism? This is because to follow these transitions in the course of their development is no longer a matter of 'naturalism'. We should be alert to the fact and remain on this side of this speculative staging. But also let us acknowledge this: can it still be a matter of what is *detached* and recognized as 'truth'—in other words, of what philosophy consummates—once there ceases to be an enigma, a question, a construction or a finality?

Let Montaigne be our witness, since we cannot hope to find a thought about ageing except by coming out of the folds of philosophy and taking a stroll in its margins. Montaigne describes life beginning with old age and as a gradual transition: 'Nature leads us down the road by a gentle slope; little by little, step by step she engulfs us in that pitiful state and breaks us in, so that we feel no jolt when youth dies in us' (1987: 101). The passage is even rougher from youth to old age, Montaigne tells us, than from old age to death: it is more 'oppressive' 'from a fresh and blooming being to non being'. Or again (the force of the gerund): 'During life, you are dying . . .'. This testimony is equally what we find in Chinese thought: life 'wears me out', says Chuang tzu, ageing 'loosens' me and death 'rests' me (Guo Qingfan, 'Da zong shi', 1983: 242). Ageing receives its legitimate place as transition— as depreciation—between the two. On the other hand, the Taoist continues, once we have stopped at the idea of death, once we make it into the Rupture and the great poignant unpacking which fixes us and no longer leaves us; as soon as we allow it to gain focus as a question, it becomes unfathomable. There is no longer an 'argument' about it: it is then absorbed into the processive nature of things and is understood in silence. As it is itself silent. Not because there might be anything ineffable or abstruse there, but because the word, as it intervenes, as it 'causes'—whether this is understood in one or another way, as transitive or intransitive— becomes a screen for this immanence.

There could be so much to learn about this passage to old age, since it is the only thing that cannot be denied; it operates on this very side of what my identity 'is' and it causes it to shatter. Because if we are not attentive about gradually raising the veil above the horizon of life, to the extent that it advances (what we commonly call experience), it will happen that this veil must one day be suddenly brutally torn away, all of a sudden, *ultimately*, causing us to fall into apocalyptic dramatizations. An external event, an encounter, a re-discovered photograph, will then suffice to bring this work of silence into prominence. But then, from being unnoticed, it becomes blinding. The 'sudden' shattering is the opposite of silent transformation. Eluding the tools of philosophy, and already in Plato (the *exaiphnes*), it now forms the object of a narrative, and literature sets it in play, making good use of its poignancy. The concluding scene par excellence—can there be any other?—is enacted in *Time Recovered*.

The short story gives an economical evidence of this (in Maupassant there are two whose titles won't mislead us, 'Farewell' and 'Finished'). The young woman who had stirred our emotions when her slender body entered the water, fresh like the wave on Etretat beach, today sits facing us in the train, stout, with her 'full-moon face', in the company of her children and beribboned, and you barely glance at her. How would I have recognized her? Faced with the decomposition of the other person, we suddenly go back, indirectly and abruptly, to our own ageing. As in a mirror, if one did not look at it every day, or rather to the photograph of twenty years earlier. 'I never had such a shock . . . I felt that a veil had been torn from my eyes'. In fact, continues Maupassant, as 'a man looks in his mirror every day, he does not see old age doing its work, for it is slow and regular, and changes the face so gradually that the transitions are imperceptible' (1970: 533, 537).

More generally, the novel, as a characteristic genre of the modern age and one which we recognize as fundamentally new, finds its function and legitimacy in narrating silent transformations. Indeed, I believe this may be its real object, notably when dealing with those great sweeping and multilayered historical transformations that set in play so many vectors and factors of the social and that cannot be contained by any single date or episode. In Stendhal's *The Red and the Black*, the ascent of Valenod and the correlative decline of de Rênal are a lot more than a backdrop. Rather, they become the subterranean transformation by which the destiny of the hero is indexed. The same thing is true for how Mme Verdurin becomes Princess de Guermantes in Proust. Tolstoy's novels are all great engines of silent transformation whose rhythms are followed by the novelist, through parallel sequences, as he passes from one character to another and then returns to them further on. We see this for instance in *War and Peace*, in how, from the lively course of brilliant action, the war is drawn out, disperses and is dissipated as the days go by to become a field of concurrent transformations before finally toppling over. Because, contrary to what is claimed about strategy as learned from Clausewitz, the 'dead time' in war, when there is no action, in which everything seems inert, where nothing 'happens' ('the phoney war'), is precisely when, in a decisive way which only becomes manifest later, the great reversals of potential and fermenting are hatched. In this regard the battles in which the subjects win distinction and think they are writing history seem no more than epiphenomena or have significance only in a consequential way.

In *Anna Karenina* we see a silent transformation of human relations. Could Anna with her decisive step and even her mischievous gesture, but whose look appears to bear a whole 'unknown world', ever have imagined that she would one day break up her household and become an outcast of society and even abandon her child, so at ease did she seem, to herself as much as to everyone else? Yet she is gradually led to it, in stages and through increasing secession, as Tolstoy attentively describes. But again, can the point of departure or the moment when her scission began be discerned? Even the thoughts of the subjects, throughout this evolution, are at best only indices punctuating a switch of allegiance which occurred much earlier; they do not even know 'when', and for a long time did not notice it. A crying out to herself, a hint of confession, certainly, but one that is not yet heard: 'why do his ears stick out so oddly?' (2003: 112) asks Anna, a precursory but nascent sign of the separation to come when she sees her husband on the platform on leaving the train.

Chapter 5
FIGURES OF REVERSAL

The transition is imperceptible, but it leads before our eyes to a complete reversal: from victory to defeat, or from love to hate, or else to indifference which is quite as much its opposite. Let's advance a step. If transformation is opposed paradigmatically to action, the transformation I call silent extends this division and makes it more apparent: would its discreet but obstinate course not be enough to challenge all of the resonant thunderclaps of Revolutions? Revolutions are loud, indeed lacerating and explosive, they most conspicuously make a breach and condense action into a frenetic contraction, or what will be described as heroic. In any case, they radicalize action and carry it to its highest intensity; it is revolutions that are consequently remembered and engraved in stone or bronze and which mark an epoch. Silent transformations, in contrast, deflect step by step—

without warning, without announcement—to the point of causing everything to topple over into its opposite without anyone having noticed.

Let us compare them both from the perspective of their results, i.e. in relation to their effectiveness or what in German is called *Wirklichkeit*. Because it forces the situation to its extreme point, intending to break forcefully with the established order, the Revolution as action, and even action carried to the extreme, necessarily gives rise to a reaction. It fights, or rather struggles, in a space of forces which have been declared and become rivals. This gives form and strength to its adversary; and even though victimized, subdued and crushed, these repressed forces no less continue to work in the shadows until they are able to flourish again. Every revolution is followed by restorations which take more or less time to arrive; but which afterwards refuse to die because the revolution has not found a point of acceptance allowing it to be integrated into its historical context. The silent transformation, in contrast, does not use force or thwart anything; it does not fight; but, as the saying goes, makes its way, infiltrates, spreads, branches out and becomes pervasive—'spreads like a stain'. It integrates as it disintegrates; allows itself to be assimilated as it takes things apart even to the measure of that which assimilates it. This is also why it is silent: because it does not give rise to any resistance to it; no one protests against it or thinks of rejecting it, no one notices its progress.

If therefore, to stick to this old image, the 'texture' of History is woven from both of them, the revolutions which are prominent, are remembered and spoken about, only represent one meshing of more brilliant visible threads set in relief on a background of the other one. Let us place these two modes of enactment side by side to test their usage. On the one side, we see that the French Revolution led, for close to a century, to a sequence of restorations and revolutions, before very gradually becoming stabilized, this time without any particularly memorable action, for the parliamentary regime came into being in an undefined and 'undeclared' way, and rather through extinction and a lack of other possibilities, corresponding to the social equilibrium and becoming thus tolerable, and even henceforth the only viable manifestation of the Third Republic. On the other side and by contrast with these spectacular bombshells, shocks and political after-effects, we notice that transformations were being propagated without alerting attention, not simply in the economic and social sphere, but also in the realms of belief and allegiance. They impose themselves without any opposition. They predispose, orient, impregnate and allow themselves to be assimilated. Anonymous and faceless—one cannot target them, still less answer them. They inflect the situation without saying a word, even to the extent of causing it to topple over, without consequently having been mastered, and without even being seen, in spite of the evidence they leave, and no one dreams of resisting them.

It is these silent transformations, more than the force of the rebellious Masses, the ultimate utopian representation of the Agent, which overturn and will overturn all the Ancient Regimes through progressive erosion of everything that supports them, in relation to which actions and revolutions are perhaps less catalyzers than simply indicators. For all that, this cannot satisfy us, and the silence of History equally keeps to its system of absorption by renewal which constitutes, if I dare say so, its 'metabolism'—for want of its Progress. Because what maintains these shadowy and silent transformations, and as a result renders History to their level, so smooth and so continuous, is that they find themselves given over to transformation in their own right at the same time as they impose themselves; they swallow themselves up as they propagate themselves or founder in their own success. The upheavals they effect in turn give birth, in the course of events, to other upheavals which integrate them in their turn, to the extent of assimilating them. Therefore, just as successful upheavals are only those that are imperceptibly prepared and silently effected, barely they have begun than they are revealed to be already committed to a fresh configuration; reabsorbed by a new gestation.

THE SILENT TRANSFORMATIONS

The rise and decline of the bourgeoisie was therefore inexorably imposed at the end of several centuries of silent transformations crowned by the Revolution, but, as it unfolded, the conditions by which this transformation triumphed bore in themselves their own interment along with their expansion. And yet is it not this very same bourgeoisie that today in its turn we see everywhere coming apart as it disintegrates under the prevailing democratization it has introduced and which has since spread so widely (not only in respect of modes of work and income, but also of access to study, ways of living, tastes, leisure and so on . . .)? Its 'death' has been clamoured (most recently in 'May 68') and now it wastes away, without our noticing it: the statue of the Bourgeois joins that of the Prince or the Hero, not having been overthrown by the anticipated Revolution, but having crumbled and come apart before our eyes, or rather melting like snow in the sunlight, from one day to the next, and, on this occasion, without a fall foretold.

But, from that point on, what is there to guide us in learning how to follow these silent transformations as they lead to a reversal, since they do not allow themselves to be reduced to securable formulae or models that could be fixed and perpetuated, and that, through each transformation introduced, there is reconfigured such a play of factors that it opens up the transformation in progress to new reorientations? No account can grasp and define this constantly renewed play of mutations.

What was it that Aristotle told us is impossible from the beginning? Precisely that there could be a 'change of the change' (*metabolé metabolès*; see Arisotle 1984b, 1068a–b: 1686–7). Since we know that according to Greek logic, as he explains it, all movement, whatever it might be, goes from one form to another, *from* something *towards* something, sup-posing by that very fact a sub-ject. At the same time if there is inversely generation from generation, or becoming from becoming, as he tells us, in other words if one generation was itself engendered then its generation must equally have been one and so on and so forth to infinity: such a becoming, he is forced to conclude, is literally unthinkable.

It is precisely here, at this stumbling block of the *logos*, that I believe Chinese culture opens up a further divergence (*écart*) with European thought, after those of Being and predication, and again offers us its resources. Are we looking for an unmodelled model of becoming, a matrix which integrates its renewal at the very heart of transformation and serves to grasp this 'change of change' that Aristotle, refusing to think *between-forms*, tells us is impossible? Let us then take from the hands of the gurus a book fundamental to Chinese civilization, the well-known *Book of Changes* or *Yi-jing* (*I-ching*), and profit from its rigour. Descended from ancient divinatory practices, it has, in fact, no other object than to train us to be vigilant and to educate our concentration: to teach us to read the gradual and continual inflections at the heart of the slightest situation by following the ways in which it splits up in proportion to how it unfolds—like the splits and cracking detected in bones or shells consigned to the fire in the earliest periods of mantic practices; and to observe the reconfigurations which result from the process each time, as they are absorbed, so discreetly conferring a new orientation to be disclosed upon the course of things.

If therefore there is indeed 'divergence' (*écart*) between China and our ancient world, we see it first in this book: a 'Classic' (*jing*), but about 'change' (*yi*). Is it even a 'book', properly speaking? If book it is, as a text that has been added to in successive layers, it is founded not on a Word but on a line: a complete or broken line (━ / ━ ━) symbolizing the two factors, *yin* and *yang*, as opposed and complementary and forming a polarity. It suggests neither a Narration, nor a discourse nor a form of reasoning, but a *dispositive*, at once aleatory and operative and, as such, to be manipulated: as they are superimposed, the horizontal lines combine into figures of three or six lines, and so they derive from one another at the same time as they become inverted when they are opposed; these oppositions assist in diagnosing, through their diagrams, the power lines at work in each situation encountered. This 'Book' consequently neither teaches a Message nor claims to deliver a Meaning (on the enigma of the world or the mystery of life, what do I know?), but examines, through rising line by line from the bottom to the top of the hexagram, how the situation is deployed and inflected in a positive or negative, or an 'auspicious' or 'ill-fated', way, in step with observed tensions and correlations and which remain in process of development (see Jullien 1993, Chapter 1).

Should we be surprised that the Chinese have consequently not been preoccupied with the Beginning and the End of things—and neither with the first beginning nor the last ending? Nor were they fascinated by the enigma of Creation, and they did not dramatize the Apocalypse: the world dies and is born every day ... This does not lead to thinking about the Eternal but, rather, about the inexhaustibility of its resources: such is the 'Sky' which, because it does not deviate from its course, is continuously engendering. Should we be surprised that the two first hexagrams of the book, which are diametrically opposed, are composed exclusively, for the first, of *yang* lines, and for the second of *yin* lines, putting in place the polarity at work in every situation, while the two last hexagrams presented in the book (63 and 64) are successively 'After' and then 'Before' the 'crossing'? In the penultimate state of 'after the crossing' (*jiji*) every line is in its place, but this perfectly adapted, and therefore ossified, order is, because of this, summoned to unravel itself; in the final hexagram, coming 'before the crossing' (*wei ji*), none of the lines are any longer in their place and a new growth is unfurled which the preceding rules do not allow to be read and which is still novel: there is therefore never a definitively completed crossing, but always a becoming of becoming and therefore you are always faced with something new to be discovered (see Jullien 1993: 141). Should we be surprised that commonly, in this context, people might speak not of 'beginning and end', but of 'end-beginning' (*zhong-shi*)? Every end is already a beginning because the transition is continuous. This is what is represented by the repeated alternation of their motifs in Chinese landscape paintings where each element drawn is, it is said, at the same time 'closed' and 'open' and which are displayed on a scroll, and absolutely not composed by a structuring of the whole picture as framed in a tableau. It is the transition that is celebrated by the emblematic bestiary of China by showing how each time has prepared its opposite: the caterpillar 'contracts with a view to extending itself' and in the same way 'dragons and snakes hibernate' 'in order to conserve their lives' (*Book of Changes*, Great Commentary B, 5).

Should we equally be surprised that the *Book of Changes* was conceived, not in the shape of Revolution, which dangerously breaks open the situation, but of Growth and Decline, such that they are inverted one into one another and one is already placed on the path of the other (hexagrams 11 and 12, *Tai* and *Pi*)? The hexagram of Growth is composed in its lower part of three *yang* lines, reflecting the Sky and, in its upper part, of three *yin* lines, reflecting the Earth (䷋) : not because the Sky is below and the Earth above and that the world is turned topsy-turvy, but because the propensity of the Sky is to rise while that of the Earth is to descend and that, so disposed, their factors encounter one another in a convergent and communicating impulse—the polarity is fully at play. The growth is that of spring, when the effluvium mingles on every side and all of nature germinates; and that of the Kingdom, when the Prince and the people are turned towards one another and remain in relations of respect or benevolence. The figure of Decline leads us to consider the opposite (☰☷): the Sky, *yang*, is taken out of its upper position and isolated on high while the Earth, *yin*, has withdrawn into a lower position, plunged in its baseness. In autumn, the forces of nature retract and dissociate; in decline, the prince lives withdrawn in his palace while the people see themselves forsaken, abandoned to their work as well as to their sorrows (see Jullien 1993: 87).

But the most important thing will be to follow from line to line how these two figures, while being opposed, pass over into each other without interruption; and even how the one already, as it unfolds, *passes into its other*. In their initial state, moreover, at the base line of the two hexagrams, the warning given is the same: it is advisable to tear up the 'reeds by their tangled roots', 'each according to its kind', in other words to unravel the confusion of the situation with which, at the beginning of growth as of decline, we are initially confronted. What is more, from before the mid-point of the Growth, it is foreseen that 'there is no flat ground which would not be followed by a slope' to be climbed; it is already necessary, in this state in which the growth has not yet established itself, to know how to locate the difficulties to come and to remain vigilant. Then, in the final line, having passed the culmination of growth (in line 5, the marriage of the King's daughter symbolizing the successful community), at its peak of the growth it is reversed of its own volition (the rampart returns to the trench): the time of enterprises is over and it is only by withdrawing into its foundations that its position could be preserved. In the state of Decline, in contrast, only the 3rd line, just before we reach the middle of the hexagram, is clearly negative. From the 4th line, we can again start to put order into the situation and recover our destiny; from the 5th line, the decline 'pauses' and we can once more attach ourselves to what is held firm by its roots and so regain our grip. Finally, the upper line of the Decline is the 'reversal' of the decline and a return to 'joy'. Therefore bad moments will never be lasting if one knows, through understanding these *transformations of transformations*, how to retain confidence. Since everything is transition, the decline itself will stagnate and new initiatives will penetrate into the shadow of the negative and be reconstituted from other forces.

Something still more decisive is involved. We notice that, in these hexagrams, it is not a particular subject, a prince or a kingdom, which has passed from growth into decline and back again. For all that, detached from the perspective of the subject, could such a reversal be described as 'structural' (according to the familiar mechanism of subject/structure)? I would describe it rather as *propensional*, on the basis that it is the situation which, by its own disposition, is *led to*; and the whole diagrammatic plan of the *Book of Changes* serves to bring to light the propensities at work in the various situations encountered. But what major displacement follows from it in the account of what happens to us (since this is the object of this Book) and constitutes our destiny? It will not fail to be manifested at the heart of the Subject and the psychological. Therefore it is not 'Me' who passes from love to hatred or indifference, but one or another feature, which at first is discreet and as if buried in the amorous relation which, as it goes on its way, is gradually led to deviate—fragmenting, undermining and re-orienting it until it is reversed. Between lovers, what at first is a fleeting divergence (*écart*) at the heart of their complicity starts to be underscored, or perhaps it begins with the first silence, which is then met with others; it concentrates, becoming more and more opaque and solid, and even henceforth becomes immoveable. They no longer have a hold over it: they have not yet noticed it, but a gulf has been opened between them.

Such a displacement forces us to reconfigure correlatively our whole notional field. I will henceforth be able to give an account of what is understood, no longer as the becoming of a subject but as the internal development of the situation, according to the propensity which is engaged in it, no longer in terms of *causality*, according to the great explanatory Greek schema, that of *aitia* but, rather, of *polarity*, in terms of these opposed and complementary hexagrams, composed of *yin* or *yang* lines, whose relation is enough to decide, in line after line, the evolution to come. Is not this displacement moreover verified in Freud when he gives an account, from his field of analysis, of the 'fate of drives', *Triebschicksal*, precisely in terms of polarity? Such is really, by virtue of the transformation of a drive into its contrary, an exemplary and even unique case, he tells us, of the 'transposition of love into hate'. But in this case why did Freud (1984) nevertheless remain more attentive to the phenomenon of ambivalence, the pure concomitance, and was barely concerned—perhaps for lack of means—to account for the collapse of one into the other?

Again, we will pass from a *personal* appreciation (concerning this or that, which we believe we can judge according to its qualities or defects) to a *configurational* appreciation of the situation encountered: therefore which features, even if they are barely outlined, dispose amorous relations to pass through one or another stage, to lean in one or another direction? We would again pass from the perspective of the *intentional*, so dear to European psychology, to that of the *functional* (*yong*, in Chinese, forming a couple with *ti*, naming the 'constitutive'):

one or another factor is at work in the situation which cannot but make their progress and unfailingly generate their effects. Finally, from an ethical point of view, we will pass from responsibility relating to culpability ('I' would be the indictable cause of this disillusion . . .) to one that takes advantage of vigilance and adaptability: in locating in time one or another negative feature as it begins to take root, I can still rectify it again by bringing it to light, as is stated at the beginning of both of these hexagrams; or rather, understanding how much it is already anchored and becomes immoveable, I deduce logically from it the evolution to come and turn myself unrepentantly towards another configuration. I have already said on this subject what everyone knows: that the lovers who accuse one another, or rather declare themselves passive and rail against destiny, are equally wrong, and that all their efforts are then in vain. They do not see that the *configuration* they form between them operates through each of them, at each moment, and is implicit in their slightest word as well as all of their silences.

Should we be surprised again that what I have translated from the Chinese up till now by 'to transform' (or 'transformation': *hua*) etymologically means to 'reverse'? According to its primitive written form, this pictogram is that of a man doubled, on the one side right way around and on the other in the inverse sense [化]. As such, its notion is coupled with that of 'modification' (*bian*) which is first of all the modification of a semitone in music and is demonstrated in practice, in the operating of the *Book of Changes*, as the substitution of a *yin* line by a *yang* line, and inversely, by going from one diagram to another. Taken together, the two terms signify the great process of the 'modification-transformation' of things as it emanates, on a larger scale, from the polarity of Sky and Earth and 'frames' all of reality; and in such a way that it is followed equally, on the individual scale, line after line, in each of these diagrams as in each situation that is encountered. Now 'to know the way of modification-transformation' according to the commentary, 'is to know what constitutes minds' (*Yi Jing*, A § 9) (or, in a more abstract way: 'what effects the dimension of mind'). It therefore comes not from the 'beyond' of this Process of modification-transformation, Chinese thought tells us, cutting short any metaphysics, nor from the religious level which eludes its mastery. For such coherence crosses the field of the visible and invisible equally; and if the 'transformation' is therefore said to be silent, it is because the slightest 'modification' that occurs is founded in the Impossible (see for example the final pages of the *Zhongyong*, § 33).

But how to think about the relation of the visible and the invisible in the way the transformation operates as it is considered to be at work within each hexagram of this book, but which also constitutes the Foundations of any reality in the eyes of the Chinese (and makes the book absolutely fundamental to their beliefs and culture)?

Employed no longer together but in parallel, 'modification' and 'transformation' express the dividing of the two. 'Modification' (*bian*) will designate the visible emergence of change, when one line is substituted for another in the hexagram, or one state of the evolution, having reached its limit, is reversed into its opposite. In relation to which, 'transformation' (*hua*) also expresses, beforehand, the still invisible maturing of the mutation that, afterwards, means that this maturing is so widespread that it is no longer seen. Thus, while the *modification* is the emerging part of the mutation, the limit being then overcome which allows a turning point or an inflexion of the process to appear, the *transformation* is the part of it that remains invisible, as much in its earlier dimension of gestation as in the subsequent phase of propagation, a phase which is also, as I have said, that of a new gestation. This transformation is consequently at once too discrete, in its play of internal influences, to appear to the outside observer, and then too extended in its results, for it to be possible still to perceive where it is different. In the first stage, as it has only made a start, the mutation is not noticed; next, as in the end it has allowed itself to be absorbed, it is no longer noticed. Between the moment when it has not yet reached the visible and that in which it will henceforth be too widely distributed and confused in the midst of the visible still to be discerned, the transformation offers only a narrow chink of perceptibility; this is why it is necessary for it to be 'examined' with so much vigilance.

Chapter 7
THE FLUIDITY OF LIFE
(OR HOW ONE IS ALREADY THE OTHER)

Let's start to recapitulate: in what respects, if we follow the logic of transformation made continuous by its progressive reversal, are we in so doing involved in a process removed from Greek thought? Because Plato also thought from contraries, but it was as a 'thing' which passes from one contrary to its contrary, or from one determination to its opposing one. He even made this a principle that he wanted to be absolutely general: 'opposites form opposites' (*Phaedo;* 1961b, 70a: 53). Because from being small I necessarily become bigger, or from sleeping I am awakened, or from living I die (and even that, from death, I live again: let's extract an argument from this, enjoins Socrates for a moment, so as to believe in the immortality of the soul). But this thesis calls for another one which completes it (after the theory of Forms is established, essences and causes separated from the empirical, at the turning point of the *Phaedo* (102–3: 83): if everything passes from one contrary into its contrary, this contrary itself will never pass into its opposite. From cold I become warm, but the Cold itself, in which I 'participate' when I am cold, will never become warm; and even whatever is possessed by the cold as an essential character—like snow—will never welcome this other into itself. But first of all it gives way at its approach since, as we have seen, these contraries are mutually exclusive. Hence, there is an inevitable rupture in the continuity of change: by participating in one and *then* in the other I 'suddenly' pass, since they do not touch each other, from one determination to what is opposed to it, as though I have exchanged them.

How is this conception separated from the one I have just started to evoke from *The Book of Changes*? In the hexagrams of this book, it is not the *self*, the prince or the people, whose growth *then* passes over into decline, but the Growth itself which, from its own determination, passes over into its contrary and goes into reverse and declines. This explains continuity by the transition of processes. Growth, in other words, does not give way at the approach of the Decline but, precisely as its development increases, it is itself already yielding towards decline. This is why, as the Growth comes to an end (in the 6th line), a manifest decline is acknowledged. As I have been expending my strength with success during the time of the Growth, I have in fact already started to wear myself out, because the more I display my capabilities, the more fragile they become, the more ground I occupy, the more I must toil to conserve it; the Roman Empire had pushed its *limes* too far not to collapse.

In a certain way, could the same thing not be said about love? The more it unfolds, the more it touches its limit. The more it culminates, becomes absolute, to the point of absorbing everything, the more it places itself in danger: feverish and intimate afternoons turn into despair to the point of suffocation. For if it is not 'me' who passes from love to abhorrence or indifference 'afterwards', is it not rather that, the more it concentrates intensity, indeed the more it puts the impossible to the test, then the closer love comes to being inverted? And so it tends to become, literally, 'catastrophic'. Moreover, it is then not a matter of 'hatred', as a feeling in the affective or psychological sense that is the opposite of love, but of the same love swinging into its negative. We know that one lover can kill the other one, due not to impulsive anger or delirium, as is too anecdotally claimed, but in a logical way—or may the amorous anger which one day arose not already have been a preliminary outline of this looming reversal?

This consequently depends upon a condition: in order for a contrary to be reversed into its contrary, it would be necessary for it already to a certain extent to contain it and implicate it. Weakness is already contained in strength and undermines it: this is why any kind of strength becomes fragile the more it is imposed, or that death is always already contained within life and develops in it. For this reason we may one day die a 'natural death'. Again, the urge towards death is not simply the other of *erôs*, as Freud goes to the point of thinking; negativity is also exercised at the very heart of the sexual impulse, even if it is undoubtedly positive, working upon it from within and prohibiting its full satisfaction (see Freud 1977; also Green 1953: 303). This moreover is what we know in a very general way about Chinese thought that has been vulgarized from *The Book of Changes*: there is already the *yin* in the *yang* and vice versa (each of two fishes represented has eyes the colour of the other, etc.). This is precisely what Plato conspicuously rejected. Thus what he was concerned with was becoming (the *genesis*), not reversal. He may have thought through the setting up of oppositions, but he excluded all logic of contradiction. Admittedly, for a moment he did touch upon it in connection with the being of non-being and when he tried to grasp the ungraspable Sophist, but he soon closed off this barely glimpsed pathway. Why?

It was because Plato took into consideration not only pairs of contraries like 'movement-rest', which we see being invoked everywhere at the start of the great explanations of the world, in Greece as in ancient China.

He also introduced 'Being' as a third term in relation to them, these contraries 'being' themselves only in as much as they participated within it (*Sophist*; 1961c, 250a–b: 994). Hence individual 'being' was prescribed, serving as a separate support with the function of a subject in such a way that it alone is what henceforth can participate in one thing and then in another, passing from one contrary into its contrary, which are held at a distance from him in their status as predicates and which leave his identity undamaged. In this way, Plato could, henceforth, use this foundation to open out the formula ('every contrary is born of its contrary') according to two distinct meanings and to decide between them: (1) a certain 'being' passes from one contrary into its opposite (which he accepts as a general rule); (2) the contrary itself passes into its contrary—which he absolutely refuses (*Phaedo*; 1961d, 103 a–c: 84). This exclusion, on which the principle of non-contradiction is founded, becomes the very rule of Reason.

It is time to point out how these Greek choices, which were thought to be purely scholastic questions, have been inscribed in European intelligence. They are not obvious and so, as they work, they have an effect, behind the scenes admittedly, but it is one that is decisive, upon the way we conceive life. It is true, if we look at it closely, that Plato did not yet discuss the 'subject' by name but, in order to distinguish contraries themselves, he calls it the 'contrary thing' (*to enantion pragma*) or 'those who possess contraries' (*ta echonta ta enantia*—those to whom are given the same names as the contraries themselves). Socrates simply introduces himself like this: I am Socrates, from being cold I become warm, from being young I become old. But Aristotle subsequently crossed this step at the beginning of his *Physics* when, as we have seen, he placed precisely the 'being' that Plato introduced as an addition to all of the pairs of oppositions 'beneath' the change, as a third term 'finding itself underneath it' (*hupokeimenon*): as sub-ject, substrate and support which therefore successively comes to be one or the other, cold then hot, young then old. Moreover, in both cases their concern is the same: to confirm not only the ontological subject, the bearer of identity (since it remains the same 'underneath' the change—at once *ipse* and *idem*—and therefore provides a guarantee of the stability of knowledge), but also as a subject of predication, a 'logical' subject, i.e. of *logos*, as support for these predicates and in such a way that it renders the deployment of the discourse legitimate. That for which Plato found the solution from the 'community' of types between them (between Being and all of the pairs of contraries, whose relations of participation must be regulated dialectically); and Aristotle in developing from that point the forms of predication that are 'categories' (in addition to 'essence', *ousia*, the basic category, these other categories which form a circle around it and determine it: quality, quantity, relation and so on).

Once again, it will be possible to make China play the role of verification *a contrario* to these Greek choices (or European *organon*) that we have assimilated so completely that we no longer discern them, even when we struggle against them. We know that European modernity was born precisely from the will to shatter this ontologico-predicative logic, the foundation of identity, in order to change the fortunes of contradiction—this has been shown for more than a century in its painting. Chinese thought has not had to construct (or has not been able to construct) a rupture of 'modernity' in the European style, like Revolt, which is also heroic and a counterforce, because it has not allowed itself be enclosed within this logic of identity, in which we see at the same time the effect of forcing and the support it offers science, at least classical science, which is that of causality: in this, would it not also have lost in inventiveness? Its logic of reversals has in any case never been disturbed and the authority of *The Book of Changes* has never been questioned. It is from Europe that China has sought to borrow its contemporary modernity and, above all, the idea of Revolution.

Moreover, the repercussions (the costs in return) from the Chinese perspective are also measured in response, i.e. in European terms: we see how Chinese thought is ill at ease (and awkward) as soon as it would like to grasp such a 'sub-ject' substrate and isolate it from the phenomenon of mutation. Even the best logician of ancient China (Xunzi, in the chapter, 'Zheng ming') could only evoke it minimally, implicitly, solely through the unique quality of 'place'. Let us then read patiently a thought which does not unfold. The only possible opposition, as far he was concerned, would be that either that 'the appearance is common' but 'in two different places', and so it would be a matter of 'two realities'; or that 'the appearance is different' but 'in a common place' and so it would be a matter of a single reality . . . According to this thinker, there is no other way of clarifying the preceding pairing of 'modification-transformation' than by considering that, if 'the appearance is modified' and the reality in question 'differs without for all that separating [into another], such is the transformation'. Obviously, if the Chinese thinker does not venture further in this direction, it is because he does not have at his disposal the concept of an identity of the subject and its ontological foundation. All the same, it still serves here as a 'pivot', he concludes, in the way of 'managing the determinisms', since such is really, effectively, in the last resort, the concern of all of the thinkers in China: not so much to think about how to develop discourse logically according to the rules of predication in order to describe the 'being' of things, than to attribute 'names' to 'things' (*ming-shi*) in a 'correct' way and to do so while respecting all the required specifications in their nomenclature. What must be avoided is making some eat into others, in a view which is consequently less speculative than fundamentally political, aiming to forbid any usurpation so as to make order reign in the Empire.

Let us return to this preliminary statement: when snow melts, it is no longer a certain 'thing', perpetuating its existence which, as support of the determinations, would change only cold's predicate. But here we have to deal properly with the *form-less*, faced with which the Greeks stopped thinking, in other words with what is no longer determined by a Form (essence) *or* by the other: is it still 'snow', but without being snow any more? Similarly, when I age, it is only within me, as a subject always identical to itself, that youth one fine day gave way to old age, for barely has old age approached than suddenly, as if by an about turn, from being 'young', I become 'old' . . . Cold no longer excludes heat, but opens the way to it. Similarly youth, far from being able to allow itself to be isolated in what would be its own character or essence, is understood only by its opposite. Does it not even already call old age the necessary result of its generous exuberance, that which it has spent without counting, without having suspected it? In the same way, as we read in the Chinese hexagrams, Growth calls towards decline and even already contains decline and reverses into it. This is why the reversal can operate continually from one state into its opposite, without being noticed. It is also why there are no ruptures in life and why transformation is 'silent'. By showing how the one passes by its own nature into its other, or how one determination becomes its opposite, and for that reason how the one is already contained in the other, the idea of reversal could not be considered, in the heart of European thought, except outside of the reign of Being and predication. This could only be before the reign had started (Heraclitus), or as it was coming to its end (Hegel).

Heraclitus did not content himself with saying, as he also said elsewhere, (2000, fragment 20: 40), that cold things get warm again and warm things turn cold, but also, in a scandalous way for the thought of Being and predication, that 'it makes no difference which is present: living and dead, sleeping and waking, young and old'. This is why, he immediately infers, 'for these changed around (*metapesonta*), are those and those changed around are again these' (ibid., fragment 13: 39). It will be noticed, in this formula, that there is no question here of subjects which happen to be one thing and then the other: they are not living beings who then become dead, or waking beings who then fall asleep or young beings who become old but, rather, they contain the contraries within themselves (in a neutral way): due to the fact of being alive or dead, awake or asleep, young or old, etc. One is thus reflected in the other and echoes back life/death, waking and sleeping and youth and old age. It is from *these determinations themselves* that Heraclitus considers what identity they possess *in* themselves (the meaning of *eni*) even through their opposition, in such a way that they are led towards reversing into one another: thus without a 'third term', in Aristotle's sense, being introduced as substrate-support of change (or sub-ject) in addition to these oppositions.

In the same way, the Hegelian dialectic gives us some clarity in this respect, not so much in its rather fastidious system by which finality would be generated as by its intelligence of the continuous passage into what is opposed to it. We know that this identity of contraries, which was first posed by Heraclitus in an immediate way, in an excessively sovereign, abrupt and condensed motion so that one could be sure of understanding it completely, Hegel for his part developed in a thorough way and, according to his own term, applied 'mediation' to it. Let us therefore return to the way in which Reason, in its progressive and painful formation, was raised from one state of comprehension to another (according to the patient itinerary described in the *Phenomenology*). An initial moment, still squeezed into the conventions of common sense and too conveniently predicative, is when determinations are perceived to be nothing but additive characteristics ('hard' 'white' 'round', etc.): they are juxtaposed at the heart of the same object as it is constructed from the 'apprehension of truth' (*Wahruchmung*), while each of them excludes its contrary and represses it ('hard or soft', 'white or black', etc.). But already, when it comes to take a force rather than a thing for an object, the mind realizes that the one is no longer simply the opposite of the other and apart from it, but that it is inseparable from it: that there is not on the one hand positive electricity and on the other negative electricity, but that one itself can be understood only through the other and that this, as we shall see later, is due to the very fact of their polarity: in this way, as force, it already contains within itself this difference of self with self—in other words, it also bears the other within the self (see Hegel 1977, Chapters 2 and 3, and the commentary in Hyppolite 1974).

When this is generalized it allows us to think not so much that things will never completely coincide with the determinations of language, so rendering their description imprecise and shifting (the well-known 'Ineffable' to which literature would be exposed), but that it is these determinations themselves which, worked upon by the other, never completely coincide with themselves (i.e. with their definition), in other words in a stable and definitive way, in spite of what common sense is tempted too complacently to believe. This is why they always find themselves swept along in a sort of passage to the borderline where each determination becomes its other. So well that both thus find within themselves the contrary of their self: 'strength', we know, finds that it is weak, 'growth' finds itself in decline. Let us therefore cease to consider these determinations, as our naive adhesion leads us to treat them, as isolatable and limited while possessing their own identity ('same as self', as Plato says about Forms [*The Sophist*; 1961c, 254c: 1000], *auto heautôi tauton*) and being walled up within their boundaries; but, if we want to think in their effectiveness, let us perceive in them the internal movement which ceaselessly discloses them and carries them towards what is their opposite. Or, from this study of strength, let us pass to the thought of 'life': if we would like to think of this movement as itself not ceasing to engender what we call 'life', or 'life as process', *das Leben als Prozeß*, says Hegel, let's refrain from fixing the determinisms by which we illuminate life as stable and definitive 'in-itself' and because of this as arrested. Equally, let's not solidify them into entities withdrawn into themselves and so inert. But let us perceive in them the 'dis-quiet' or non-rest, *Unruhe*, which continues to disappropriate them from within and invert them, finding 'infinities' within them. Concerning life, this is really its very essence where its 'fluidity', *Flüssigkeit*, is found, which is, properly speaking, a non-essence: that is why also we have so much difficulty in thinking about it.

When we set that machine in motion again, the one that can now grind everything up in its path, of the dialectic, to set in play this 'auto-movement' again, whose gears no longer grate, of a reversal that has come into force as though it were automatic, one could almost forget what these Hegelian terms have nevertheless found for us that is crucial, in their logical effort to come to the end of the romanticism of their youth, as Jean Hyppolite would recall in this respect, that is effectively *vital*: that, for whoever wants to enter into the silent transformations of life, the 'thingism' to take apart is not so much that of our perception of things themselves, which is so easy to set about, than that of determinations by which our mind claims to grasp them; and that it tends to fix. Or that, to think about how to pass from the discontinuity of purely successive states to the continuity of a process, effectively calls for nothing less, as Hegel wanted, than to conceive of negation in a quite different way. Let us therefore no longer hold on to negation as a limit that is *external to determination*, as classic philosophy did, distinguishing it only from all other possible determinations (in *The Sophist*, 'non-being' is not the contrary but everything that is other than Being) and so not casting doubt on the very being of this determination which, as such, remains in complete adequacy with itself and retains an indestructible internal positivity. What can alter or disturb a being determined in this way (cries, lacerations and even death) could not from that point occur within it except as an alien event producing the internal rupture. But let us conceive of this negation as working in the very interior of the determination: breaking this adequacy (what Hegel calls 'equality') of the determination with itself and therefore finding it contradictory in itself—and therefore already on the point of being reversed.

Can I, in fact, take a determination only for what it 'is': 'strength' only as strength, and 'weakness' only as weakness, each of them withdrawn into themselves and coinciding with their definitions? But how can we not see that any position (determination) of 'strength' is already in itself worked upon by weakness and finds itself to be undermined by it? This means that each of these contrary determinations, as they develop, are finally to be reversed into the other; and thus rendered as *continuous*, i.e. without true rupture, even for Revolutions (as the dialectic of Master and Slave continues to teach us). Strength exhibits and imposes itself and, by this very fact, as I have already said, it makes itself weaker; and it is even the case that the more it imposes and proves how strong it is, the weaker, or the more guilty (see Nietzsche), it becomes. This is the ineffable weakness of leaders. And the inverse is equally true: the strength of the weak, of those one does not even dare touch, is such that they take advantage of the fact, so much do they allow their weakness to appear incontinent: the weakness they display is therefore reversed, into a strength that is all the more effective because it has not had to be assumed or admitted as such, but has remained under cover and withdrawn. Is this not the tyrannical power that children often assume at the heart of families? Or what the tearful lover wants to remind you about through her tears? There is another example I hardly dare advance since the determinisms in this case seem so ideologically fixed, defended as they are by good conscience. This is the 'untouchability' by which (as is proved to us every day?) so-called 'subaltern' categories or once scorned social groups are equally able to prevail: more effectively than anyone, they can (like civil servants) claim from the outset to be understaffed, overworked, exploited, lacking respect and so on, and on principle to be so badly off that we are always afraid of bothering them and that any action on their behalf appears to be a service . . . They make themselves a rampart, rendering themselves impregnable, from the spectacle of their 'weakness'; indeed have a hold over others by retaliation under cover of this determination.

Henceforth, our error, from which comes our lack of intelligence about life, is that we consider these determinisms to be immoveable, instead of keeping them 'fluid'. Still more, we tend to engage with these determinations as solid blocks upon which our beliefs and convictions depend, without seeing how, under cover of their fixity, the situation could be radically changed with all the more impunity for its not having been announced. And, for our part, we are all the less in a position to account for such a reversal of the situation, even when it is present, glaringly, right in front of us, due to the fact that we remain attached to these blocks of immobility in order to describe it. They impress it upon us. In this way, an Ideal is dogmatically maintained, firm on its foundation and consigned to currying favour with the public, although it is already completely devoid of substance and finds itself abandoned. Indeed, it becomes, under cover of these determinations, more oppressive than any overt oppression.

Such is the everlasting history of religious fervours surreptitiously reversing under an ideological screed, or of Revolutions swinging without warning towards reaction. For once again, can we ever say when (and from what point) such a swing has started? We still believe in these 'progressive' forces and forms because they bear this determination as their standard, and display them as such, that we take pride in their definition and fail to perceive how much, under cover of the same emancipatory slogans, their 'engagement' has been inverted and no longer defends ideals, but from that point on what has been 'acquired'. It has ceased to be a vector of heroism (for the emancipation of the oppressed) but is now one of egoism (through corporate interest). It no longer confronts a real danger (in challenging Power at the risk of one's life), but has sunk into the comfort of conformist demands and so on. Social forces are no longer innovative but have become fossilized, factors of mobility have reverted to immobility and yet remain above all suspicion, since the determinisms demanded are the same and lead us to believe in the permanent nature of their content. Take, for example, nineteenth- century trades' unionism (emancipatory and courageous) with, I would suggest with no malicious intent, a certain trades' unionism of today.

Transformations are therefore silent not simply due to their mode of emergence (from a point of view we will call phenomenological) but also because they are infinitely gradual and not local but global, unlike action, and thus do not differentiate themselves, nor are they noticed in consequence (just as 'everything' ages within us and in the duration, we do not see ourselves becoming old . . .). This is so not simply because these transformations do not allow themselves conveniently to be grasped by our logical ontological-predicative tools, distributing determinations in a chain to a 'sub-ject', in an attributive way: no matter how many predicates we vainly string one behind another, we would still not have started to enter into what constitutes the experience of ageing. The transformations (inversions) are silent in a still more insidious, and crafty, way, supported by our very usage of language. Because we isolate the opposing determinations 'youth' and 'old age' or 'strength' and 'weakness', or 'life' and 'death', from one another, freezing each one in its definition and solidifying it in its essence, and because we hold each one apart from the others, so, under what are now only fixed determinations, the passage from one to the other slips away—and once more we find ourselves with empty hands.

We are then tempted to recover what eludes us about this continuity of transition separately by naming it in a unitary way as 'time' and, by having introduced ruptures that became necessary in our description of the change which affects it, in whose heart we reside and which we call 'events'. But why defer to Time, modelling it once more as an external authority and great Agent, which we could grasp sufficiently from the very interior of the process? Having reached this point of disturbance of our conceptions, I cannot avoid this most significant question. Would Time not be what we have constructed as an alibi, admittedly a hypostatized and ennobled one, as a great Subject which is responsible for everything and from the outset can be so conveniently invoked, so avoiding our incapacity to bring attention (dependant as we are on the authority of language and its fixations) to this 'silence' of transformations?

Chapter 8
WAS IT NECESSARY TO INVENT 'TIME'?

A distressing paradox of language is that the mind develops and we are able to think thanks to language and through its means. At the same time, to think is always, in one way or another, to turn against language and struggle against submission to it: to make every effort to loosen ourselves from its constrictions and, detaching ourselves from what it most obviously imposes upon us (nothing is more suspect than 'evidence' in philosophy . . .), to try to return prior to its old carving up. I have refrained until now from invoking 'time', even though I want to speak about change, because I think that 'time' is a construction of language, and more especially of European language, which to a large extent deceives us and deflects us from the logic of processes. We have, from the time of the Greeks, packed into the term 'time', *chronos*, everything we are no longer able to justify from our notional distributions and disjunctions, and we erect it as a hegemonic and enigmatic Cause of our lives. This prompts a question which, at this point of reflection, I must now risk advancing: is Time not that character of a dramatic fiction we have invented in order to give a name and a face to what we are unable to think, and to make it play a great, and undoubtedly widespread, explanatory role, one from which a more painstaking attention to silent transformations would have excused us? For it makes common cause with this Greek choice *par excellence* that is our choice of Being and throws in its lot with it, by recovering what the thought of Being has abandoned, in a way so as to serve as a frame and support for the 'becoming' confronting it. 'Being and Time', *Sein und Zeit*, is by its conjunction a generic title for European thought in its entirety.

Once again we could develop an argument from Chinese language and thought, because the Chinese language has never spoken of 'time' in a unitary and general way. On the one hand it speaks of the moment-occasion, the 'season' (*shi*) which through its variation measures the life of things, induces our activities and serves as a framework for ritual: evoking through writing the germs of life contained on the earth and that the sun makes radiant, the term retains and is profoundly anchored in a qualitative and circumstantial meaning. On the other hand, it speaks of 'duration' (*jiu*) which proceeds from the alternation of such moments and is paired with space (notably in the *Mohist Canon*; see Graham 1978: 293).

The proof lies in the fact that from the late nineteenth century, upon encountering Western thought, the Chinese have translated 'time' as the 'between moments' (*shi-jian* in Chinese; *ji-kan* in Japanese). Until then they thought both about seasonal variation and the duration which flows from it, but never isolated a homogenous-abstract time from the duration of process. When the possibility was at times sketched out, through the evocation of a moment that is no longer seasonal but durative (see, for example, Guo Qingfan 1983: 568), as I have had occasion elsewhere to examine (Jullien 2001: 44), we still never see this process come to a conclusion, and this is because it was not driven to play a very decisive explanatory role.

The Chinese have nonetheless calculated the moments of the day, the years or the eras with precision. They have nonetheless created very elaborate clocks, notably using hydraulic functioning, and have been especially rigorous in the elaboration of their calendars. They have in particular devoted all their attention upon History, a founding knowledge in China, and they have with extreme care drawn up chronologies making room for dynastic synchronicities. From this, an argument has been put forward that they consequently must have had an 'implicit' concept of 'time', analogous to the European but that European thought alone would have developed, because was the latter not above all universal and necessary, a sort of *a priori* of thought? (See, for example, Harbsmeier 1995: 49 or Wu Kuang-ming 1998: I discuss these conceptions in Jullien, 2001: 35.) But besides the fact that it is difficult to see why the Chinese should not themselves have developed a concept of time, since their thinking is as equally elevated in abstraction, we notice only too well, as soon we follow the divergences manifested between the cultures, how Greek thought had to expand upon eminently singular preconceptions and why Chinese thinking felt able to dispense with them.

Greece had at least three reasons for having to think about time, which China passed aside. The first of these points of entry is related to the preconceptions of its physics (see Aristotle, *Physics*, IV) which, in its approach to 'nature' (*phusis*) as a body in motion, caused 'time' to intervene in order to account for the displacement of a moving body from point A to point B, points of departure and arrival, as we have seen, as a 'numbering of movement according to a before and an after'. But China has approached what we call 'nature' in terms not of a body in movement, or as elements, but as factors in correlation (*yin* and *yang*) from whose polarity all engendering stems. Faced with this there is another starting point in Greek thinking about time, a rival for the first, and relating to its metaphysics, which opposes time to eternity: no longer as a divisible and continuous magnitude, but under the conjoined aspects of endless succession and alteration. While only Being is eternal, 'since it always exists', *aei ôn*, all 'becoming' is in time, a 'moving image' of eternity (at least, if we read the formula in this way) from which time has 'fallen' (Plato-Plotinus). In contrast, China has thought not about the 'eternal' of that which would always be identical with itself, but about the 'without end' or the 'inexhaustible' (*wu qiong*), allowing the quality invested to be renewed without ever being exhausted—such as the 'Sky' which the Chinese regarded as the Foundation of the Process of things.

Finally (but perhaps this should come first of all?), European languages conjugate. They morphologically divide up the tenses among themselves (past/present/future) and thus conceive of time from the outset as a passage from one tense to another. These pass 'from' the future 'through' the present and 'into' the past, said Augustine, reproducing questions of place in Latin (*unde*, *qua*, *quo*) to think about time—the fourth case, *ubi*, the place 'where one is', or rather where God 'is', being reserved for eternity. In contrast, the Chinese language does not conjugate: it possesses possible markers of the past and the near future, but it does not distinguish specific times by conjugation. Its basic representation in this respect has moreover two terms rather than three (polarity once again) which I will translate most literally as 'going away: past/present: coming here (*wang gu jin lai*). The past is endlessly going away/ the present is endlessly coming here. It is a return to the transition. (On these three entries into the question of time see Jullien 2001, Chapter 1.)

Not passing through these (European) points of entry into the question of time, Chinese thought precisely has not had to make time into a 'question'. In order to test its consistency, it has examined the proceedings of things as well as how they are conducted, their procedures and their processes, their propensities and the way they are used (what is generically called *tao* in Chinese), and it has done so from the smallest to the greatest scale, the duration of a life or a world. But for all that it has not posited 'time' as that which has enveloped them all and, detaching itself at once from their duration and their simultaneity, would constitute an entity fit to serve as an *a priori* framework for our perception of change (or *a priori* form of our sensibility, according to Kant). European thought, in contrast, has not dreamt of challenging the necessity of thinking about time, but makes it the question *par excellence*, or rather an enigma. Because, as Aristotle had already established, time is 'divisible', but its divisions do not exist (it is a *meriston* without *mérè*) and we must really assume a certain reality for it since it is then divided up (between different times: past/present/future) but one is obliged also to recognize that none of these divisions really exist, since 'being' does not correspond to any of the three: the future 'is' not yet, the past 'is' no longer, and the present 'is' nothing but the point of passage from the future into the past and has itself neither extension nor, consequently, existence. The reality of time is thus inevitably 'obscure', Aristotle concludes (1984a 218a: 370); and each great philosophy, in Europe, has been unable to do otherwise than redeploy the question with a view to illuminating in its own way this fascinating obscurity. Would this question then not constitute from the outset an impasse—'an aporia' in the literal sense—against which European thought has fought, even in a sublime way, assuredly, but without ever escaping it? How then has it happened that we have had to invent it?

I say we have 'invented' the question of time because we see clearly that it was born from a long process of trial and error at the heart of Greek thought, even before philosophy had become established and had taken possession of it. Let us remember that in neither Homer nor Hesiod does 'time' ever appear as the subject of a verb, but simply designates the wait upon which success or failure depends and distinguishes the outcome; and that, in both of them, the course of the 'days' (*émar*) is qualitatively perceived as favourable to one or another activity (Onians 1955: 485) in a way that on the whole is close to that of the ancient Chinese. It is therefore through 'logical' rewriting of primitive cosmogonies (i.e. gradually passing from the *muthos* from the *logos*), that Time assumes such a characteristic authority, instigated together with Zeus and the earth, Zas and Chtonié (in Pherekycles), and posed as subject and Grand Agent (Diels-Kranz 1952, VOL. 1: 47). To what extent is he then confused with his homonym (but for one letter), Kronos, the god who devours his children? By what filiation is he equally linked with the mysteries of Orphism? Is it still the case that from that time the Gnomics and the Tragedians describe him as the one who is 'wisest', who 'discovers everything', or who 'shows the truth', or 'reveals things' (Thales, Solon, Theognis)—and he is made absolute as the all-powerful Authority. The 'Father of all things', says Pindar (see Fraenkel 1955: 112; Romilly 1995, Chapter 2): conceived as engendering himself, he becomes the principle of a continuous renewal, independent of events themselves and giving birth to them. Time begins to be spoken of more currently as what 'passes', 'approaches' or 'elapses', etc. These expressions which we have since repeated every day, without thinking about it, as though they went without saying, show the extent to which they have been assimilated but which become again the source of an infinite perplexity, as Augustine noted, as soon as one stops to think about them.

In fact, in its way taking over from Olympian deities, 'time' is no longer experienced as a totally external being, but for all that is not completely internalized; it is said, rather, for the Tragedians, to be in transition from one to the other, standing 'beside' us and accompanying us. A strange character, after all, one who is discreet, remains in the background, but with whom we live together and to whom our life is joined but not yet assimilated: it 'sleeps with me', says Clytemnestra before committing the murder, it informed me 'in being with me', together with my sufferings, says Oedipus, at the twilight of his life ... (Aeschylus 1956: 73; Sophocles 1982: 283). Because, if it serves as a purified and demythologized figure of transcendence, Time no less still preserves the status of a person, and will even henceforth ceaselessly oscillate between one and the other pole, between abstraction and personification. In testimony, we can take Anaximander, for whom it is 'according to the assignation of time' (*kata ten tou chronou taxin*) that the necessity of becoming is first established, in step with which beings appear and disappear indefinitely, rendering each other in this way, as they succeed one another, 'justice and reparations for each of them' (Diels-Kranz 1952, VOL. 1: 86). 'According to the assignation of time' here means at once the temporal order and the verdict of the judge reigning over continual births and deaths, generations and corruptions. With Anaximander the assimilation of becoming and Time, which will impose thinking 'according to' the dimension of Time which constitutes existence upon the whole of European culture, is sealed.

When the *logos* of philosophy comes to prevail, it can thus do no more than inherit this hypostasized Time as an autonomous and dominating authority over beings. More precisely and in a more sovereign way, it even becomes the 'being' of being. This is even so for the least mythological of Greek thinkers, Aristotle. After he conceived of time analytically in its function as a measure, in relation to numbers, his sudden reflection *ultimately* topples over (Aristotle 1984 a, 221a: 374): at the point when he considers that, for all things, 'to be in time' is to be measured by time, not only in its movement but equally in its 'being', *kai to einai*. Why this slippage? Why, from movement's numerical nature, must time become that 'by which the 'existence of things' in general is measured, if not because the analysis of physical time is found to be swamped, even in Aristotle, by this cultural representation of a guardian Time, recovering under this abstract mode the all-powerful nature of the religious? And from this to consider, by means of a properly meta-physical exceeding, a time 'greater than everything which is within time', according to Aristotle's own terms, 'enveloping' everything and serving as a framework to all existence; and, what is more, to be tied once more to the personified conception of Time erected as great Agent and 'cause in itself' of the destruction which, as Aristotle notes, we 'have the habit of saying', that it 'consumes': that all ageing occurs 'through it', that everything is erased 'through it' and that only 'eternal beings' escape from it since they are 'not within time'.

Why has it never occurred to European thought—when it has made so much effort throughout its history in refusing to accept its assumptions and to be self-critical, which has always, in other words, broken with its own conceptions and disentangled itself—to emerge from this impasse of 'Time', rooted as it is in language, but which we can easily see how singular and culturally marked it is in comparison with China: from this conception of 'Time' caught in the metaphysical opposition between Being and becoming as well as in its widespread explanatory role as all-powerful Subject serving as the ultimate avatar of the Divinity? We never find any Chinese author, at least before China encountered Europe and the concept of time became globalized, saying that time 'does' this or that; or even simply that 'time passes'. But do we not know, as Ronsard has poetically described for us, that it is not time but, rather, 'ourselves' which 'pass': that there are, on a more or less broad scale, only individual processes of transformation? Equally, we will not find a Chinese author saying, as we commonly do, following Pascal (and even Proust 1981: 321), that 'time heals pains and quarrels' (Pascal 1966: 269). We know perfectly well, just as much as Pascal, that it is we, as individuals, who change and that 'pains and quarrels', like loves, are borne along by themselves, in other words by their propensity to turn of themselves into indifference, or rather, to wear themselves out in the long run.

Have we not therefore erected Time as a total Subject, easily assignable and therefore conveniently invocable because, for want of according a sufficient status to silent transformations, we needed to invoke a Great Agent to account at the same time for the emergence of things into the visible and for their invisible reabsorption; or which, as a hero in Sophocles said about this 'long' and even 'unmeasured' pulse of time: 'Revealing what is hidden' and 'then shrouding what appears' (Sophocles 2007: 31)? The most general ostensible cause, because it is detached from singular evolutions, but of which we have also known that, since the time of the Greeks, as soon as we think just a little about nature and shift from the comforts of language, we once again fall into aporia. Is it not equally the case that we have been able to reinvest the old religious anguish by which European tradition has dramatized existence in the thought of a destructive Time and which, under the personified figure of Time, as already found in Anaximander, that tradition likes to evoke in 'more poetic words' (*poietikôterois onomasin*): Time 'eats away life' (Baudelaire). It is that 'dark Enemy who guides our hearts', 'on blood that drips into his jaws' (1993: 178).

Nevertheless, we could equally, by following the 'modification-continuity' of things and situations, as we learn to do in going back to *The Book of Changes*, 'tend towards the seasonal moment' (*bian-tong qu shi*; Grande commentaire, B 1) as this book says and, making oneself available to it, live in phase with its recurrence. Rather than throwing oneself 'towards' the End, rushing towards the future because we 'lack being', as Plotinus rightly said, and 'drawing from being to self' (*elkôn to einai hautôi*) in always making 'something else and still something else' (Plotinus, 1992: 72). To such a running ahead, the *Vorlaufen*, from which Heidegger constructed the ontological structure of 'existence', thereby sealing the tragic orientation of European thought, one can then oppose this *availability* of 'living' finding its 'stability' (serenity) in the 'moment' (*an shi*, as the Zhuangzi says; Guo Qingfan 1983: 128 and 260) and 'conforming with it'. To live 'in time', as Montaigne, that thinker of occurrence and transition, likewise said, rather than in the anguish of an impossible present, however true it may be that the 'present', which alone is 'being in front' (*praes-ens*), is nevertheless only a point of passage and is even infinitely divisible—not even an 'atom' of time—and never 'exists'.

What need therefore did Proust himself have to settle all accounts by taking back, under the simultaneously inclusive and legendary figure of Time, the innumerable silent transformations which, one by one, revealed themselves to the Narrator, to the end of all the years that passed, as he spent his final morning with the Princess? For how does making Time into an invisible 'essence' that is suddenly revealed, *in fine*, as a kind of theophany, a literary continuation of the Last Judgement, serve as any kind of explanation? How does going from the absolute quality of Being to that of Time, so bartering one metaphysic for another, and consecrating what changes rather than what is stable (privileging drama over repose), constitute an advancement of our modernity? Because there is still nothing there, right in front of us, in the lounge of a Parisian hotel, encountered in that final meeting, but individual and discreet processes of ageing which are slower for some, more striking for others, and whose results can be evaluated only after the event, on the occasion of this great Return; or the 'reversals' of 'situation' (Proust 1981b: 406), which, echoing those greater ones of History, led the Prince de Guermantes, having been ruined by the war, to marry Madame Verdurin, or Rachel to receive the applause that should have been for the actress La Berma. Or else the very subtle modifications of emotions when the Narrator finally realizes that Albertine, whom he once held 'dearer than his life', has become a matter of indifference to him. The force of silent transformation, an insidious force, lies in its managing to make something go without saying today, completely absorbed by the situation and happening without a word, without being noticed, that thing which we would earlier have so strongly denied, so impossible would it have seemed . . . Even to the extent that we would have been unable to imagine it.

Why do we therefore assume that all of these phenomena, various and concurrent as they are, as we have recourse to the old descriptive ontological formulae, are based upon the same subject-substrate-support which is Time, as a unique Agent, one that is definitively hypostatized and that subsumes without further resistance all of these different changes—a 'Time' that is still and always personified? Why is it therefore necessary to add this phrase that hides in such an awkward way the psychological, not to say neurotic, transfer of which Time is always the object: '[...] But there was a more serious reason for my distress. I made the discovery of the destructive action of Time' (ibid.: 298)? Yes, why, still and perpetually refurbishing it with such 'poetic words', as can already be found in the great fragment of Anaximander, according to the quotations, the only evasion found in the aporia of the discourse-reason, representing Time as an artist who glues 'masks' onto faces or who paints his 'models', that are still recognizable but no longer faithful representations? Or to describe the young woman who has become matronly as being like a clumsy swimmer scarcely able 'to move through the waves of time' which overwhelm her (ibid.: 308)—thereby dramatically awakening the old but still unsteady image according to which, just as in space, each person might occupy a place 'in Time' (the final words of *Time Regained*).

One might retort that a time really does exist from which lives are made, and that this is undeniable because its nature is physical. But precisely we notice that physicists have been increasingly careful, at least since the era of Newton, to 'reduce' the notion of time by separating *time* and *becoming* from one another. On the one side is the 'course of time' by which the present moment is renewed, and in such a way that it organizes a successive continuity, an always unique moment which is never represented twice ('the postman of time never rings twice' as Étienne Klein says): 'this time' produces nothing more than duration. This 'time' is sufficient, we are told, for physics (2007).[1] On the other side is to be placed what we have habitually called the 'arrow of time', which is not related to time itself but to what develops in its core and which is therefore not an attribute of time but a possible (irreversible) property of phenomena. It is this temporal 'arrow' which alone constitutes becoming, the change that affects beings. The error of common language, as physicists also tell us, is to attribute to time itself the characteristics of temporal phenomena which have been placed there by us; in other words, to confuse 'time' with what occurs within it. Physics recognizes only the course of time divested of everything that occurs for us, that is independent of everything that happens in it and whose structure guarantees all moments the same status. Yet it is only according to the temporal arrow of phenomena, constituting their becoming, which is of no interest to physics, that 'events' can be understood.

Note

1 I should like to thank Étienne Klein for his help when we discussed this subject.

Chapter 9
MYTHOLOGY OF THE EVENT

An event, in fact, is not just any moment but one that becomes prominent and is detached in relation to the continual renewal from which duration is born. In attributing it with a specific being, one that can not only be isolated but is also self-consistent ('what an event!...'), in other words in recognizing that it has the capacity to produce 'itself', as though it bears within itself an initiative or at least its own individuality, we cause it to introduce a flaw into the continuity of change, while all of the adjacent moments are forced back into the darkness, as secondary and dependent. Not only is it exceptional but it also gives rise, in its irruption, to an upheaval whose consequence reconfigures all of the possibilities invested in it. When we say that something 'happens', it always implies a breaking open which results in an overflowing (exceeding) of the present moment: 'It seems,' wrote Proust in *The Captive*, 'that events are larger than the moment in which they occur and cannot confine themselves in it' (1981a: 540). This is why, no matter how anticipated the event may have been or how justified it was afterwards, or how explicable it might become in its context, it contains something inassimilable—or highlights an element external to it—which transcends any simple causative explanation and calls for the aid of an interpretation: so much would the enigma of its origin still remain fascinating. Its apparition is to be 'deciphered', as phenomenologists like to say, while never completely renouncing the language of epiphany.

I have come to have doubts about this: does such an event really exist, that is other than in the form of a fictive or mythological representation? Would it not rather be, like a line of foam, nothing but the visible emergence of transformations that remain as invisible as the deeply buried movements of a breaking wave of water? It is true that we speak of the event, and even that we speak of nothing else, or that, expressed the other way round and already as equivalent to a definition, that just speaking about it no sooner 'creates an event'. But, if they divide the spheres of the word and silence between them in this way, the event monopolizing attention and the transformation being too diffuse, widespread and continuous, to what extent does the event still need to be conceived of as the epiphenomenal budding of transformation (the eruption of what has for so long been brewing) if it is not to go unnoticed? That is to say, to what extent is the event actually an abrupt *springing up*, as the word itself expresses it (*e-venit*), rather than a *maturation*? Or to what extent is it to be conceived as an *encounter* (with what the latter assumes about the External, and even with what cannot be integrated) rather than as a *result*?

We know the objection to this that has always been invoked: love . . . Is not love the sudden, unforeseeable encounter whose appearance upturns everything? Another man or woman needs to cross our path, arising from elsewhere, and bringing this elsewhere with her or him. Is not the 'bolt from the blue' that is love at first sight the ingress which suddenly breaks with the whole past by opening up other, completely new, possibilities? How could we have even the slightest intimation of its coming? That, upon leaving the train one morning, Anna Karenina will meet Vronski is the event which, overflowing the moment, causes the disruption of her whole life . . . Nevertheless, is this really what Tolstoy wrote? Was he not careful to show, under Vronski's searching gaze, that a contained vivacity flutters through her physiognomy which gives rise to the suspicion that there is a repressed force within her, some 'inner fire', I recall, which cannot be consummated but which has increased in a barely perceptible way, which is there waiting, and which demands not so much a reason as a support, a pretext, in order to be ignited? In Anna's alert and determined step there is more than spirit and vivacity. Something already reveals itself in pointing towards that epoch in which disappointment with her life as a woman has silently yet inordinately increased, even though she has not yet come to the end of her youth.

For such an 'event' to be possible (for her to fix first her look and then, soon after, her entire life on Vronski), conditions have to be ripe, which demands that the bored flesh is finally stirred and that too many superficial conventions, so heavy as to be unbearable, dramatically tip over into an open rupture. All in all, Vronski is therefore only the indicator or the trigger—the fortuitous cause, as theologians would say—of the 'overwhelming' need to love, in other words to give access to the other without counting the cost, which the young woman had contained within herself for years and who had until that moment deported herself as best she could, for want of burying herself completely, indeed that she has kept masked from herself under her elegant reserve. Evidence is provided by the fact that Vronski, in spite of his good will, will never meet it, and that, as in all true stories, she will remain walled up and alone in her love, which will be silently inverted as the turmoil of seduction turns into solitary suicide. Each of them is an object of investment for the other, indeed soon of every investment, but their two stories, as they each follow their own logic by night, and beyond interference, will remain parallel.

9/11 could equally be invoked. Was that not the brutal event *par excellence*, which overturned the history of the world and of which no one, not even those who planned it, could anticipate all that it would give rise to, or how much it would introduce new possibilities? But here again I believe it will be possible to reverse the perspective, because was not this—an event if ever there was one—rather the visible, sonorous and even spectacular 'emergence' of the transformation that remains silent, precisely because it was global, and that for once is rightly called by the name of 'globalization'? Could one seriously imagine, in a sort of optimism born from the Enlightenment, the last 'Wall' having fallen and all nations from now on conferring together, that the negative would definitively withdraw on tiptoe from History, a History that would be over because it had been forever pacified? I would believe instead that this negative, at work throughout history and which *never vanishes*, and which is no longer today allowed to be aimed outside (globalization suppressing this Outside) because it belonged to another camp or another class (as between the USA and the USSR at the time of the Cold War), naturally came to be internalized and that, ceasing to have a head-on, demarcated and open outlet, it could therefore only take an occult form which would cease to be confinable but become disseminated (and be returned without warning) by 'terrorism'.

THE SILENT TRANSFORMATIONS

Global transformations, indeed, and ones which have consequently ceased to be prominent: economic interests being henceforth too narrowly entangled in the same 'world' by the laws of the market, ruptures are progressively led to re-form on another level which has become that of belief and values, in other words where the ideological can be once again asserted in full autonomous right—hence the recrudescence of dogma, sacrifice and triumphant Faith. These are all the more strongly inclined to parade their intransigence by violence, because they can brazenly oppose the desperately feeble, when it is not openly hypocritical, discourse of international cooperation, i.e. that of unanimously broadcast and 'completely positive' feelings. I do not therefore deny that 9/11 has been magnified, in its consequences, from a brutal mutation of relations of force and political conduct, but I also believe that it is observable as the fruit of a reconfiguration and *silent maturation* of the negative which also possesses, in parallel with this sudden irruption, its endemic manifestations (like the war in Afghanistan) but has remained in this particular case hidden under the sensationalism of the Event and its effect of dramatic condensation.

The event is not simply what monopolizes the attention; it also structures the narrative and serves its dramatization, which means that it is really the constitutive element of a *muthos*. Because it has elaborated its basic representations with the aid of Grand Narratives, and thus in a mytho-logical way, European culture could be defined, I believe, as a culture of the Event. The event holds a prestige which it has never renounced due to the rupture it has effected and all of the unprecedented things it has opened up, because of what it allows by way of focus, and consequently of tension as well as *pathos*. It has never been able to renounce it because it is avidly (passionately) attached to the fascinated-inspiring character of the event. Is not its very belief formed of absolute events? The Eternal here crosses paths with the temporal, and the breaking open is then total: Creation, Incarnation, Resurrection and so on. And this is because Christianity is that strange religion in which, since its prophet is God on earth, His life becomes the Event cutting off all of History and configuring Time. In our literary staging as well, everything has contributed to emphasize the appealing and captivating vertigo of the event. Whether we are speaking of Homer or Pindar or the Tragedians, all of them aim to produce an irreducible event which does not allow itself to be understood within the memorable framework of cycles and episodes, and would be the particular case of nothing more general: an incomparable, non-integratable event, carried as far as possible—the source at the same time of incessant sublimation and questioning.

In this way, serving best of all the ideology of rupture which is so dear to Europe, the event still continues to fertilize philosophy today. When Alain Badiou considers that what is gathered together for the 'composition' of a Subject must necessarily *also* intercede to the given objective, in other words 'occur' in situations in a way that these situations themselves would be unable to account for, and that what he calls an 'event' is this supplement, by contrast with the dismal inertia of circumstances, he remains squarely in the wake of that European mythology which makes the event the only path by which to force an entry into what has been conditioned, and therefore is an affirmation of Freedom (see Badiou 2005; also Badiou 2000 and 2003). This serves to invest the Revolution with the path (very well described by him nevertheless) from which the apostle Paul constructed the coming Event (of) Christ. In order for a 'subject' to be constructed let us suppose it to be necessary that, going beyond the animality it is, something happens that is irreducible to its ordinary inscription in the 'there it is'; and let us consequently consider that it is the decision alone henceforth to relate to the situation from the point of view of exigency that constitutes this event-related supplement, in other words in 'fidelity' to this event, that a process of truth emerges as the sole foundation of ethics. In this case, does one not once again make the rupture opened by the Event the condition of a promotion of 'existence'? The continuity which results in the fact that there really is a great tradition in Europe, even beyond its inveterate myth of Rupture, indeed beyond the end of the Grand Narratives, that depends less probably on the religious message itself than on the means of bringing to light, through the aberrant prominence of the Event, that other level of the unprecedented, or of the new, in other words of what is irreducibly other in relation to invested situations which perpetually depend on the 'miracle'...

I understand that, by contrast, phenomenologists are still fascinated by this non-integratable emergence of the event, in which they see the 'phenomenon' *par excellence*, the better to be in a position to bring appearance to light, and therefore the most revealing, or rather the only revealing thing in itself, from which consequently the phenomenological concern can no longer be detached. They too want to liberate language: to think of change without the 'thing' upon which change is pre-supposed; and, for that reason, to free the statement from the change of predicative structure that assigns it to a subject, making it from the outset pass under the thumb of Being and causality. This would require it not to hold onto the verbalization of the event (the 'arrival', 'emergence', 'happening'...) in the dependency of the Agent and the substantive but, rather, to invert the mutual relations beneath them, since it is 'illumination' that gives birth to clarity, as Claude Romano points out in a beautiful book (1998), and that clarity is its only result. To understand once more the accession of the world in each singular event, this 'world' itself opening and deploying itself only within them, would come at this price—it is at this price that the 'originating' would be rediscovered.

However, what could result from this claim of a pure verbality (activity) affirmed against the reigns of Being, the substantive and the subject, since this claim is the very one which founds rights apart from the event, once we have emerged from the morphology of our language? What happens when we pass into a language, like the Chinese, in which, as I have noted, the same word can be verbal, nominal and adjectival? Starting with their theory of the 'intangible' as reconfiguring its causality, the Stoics effectively developed a propositional status of the event which releases it from its predicative dependency; but they did so by anchoring it even more in its difference between the noun and the verb, the *onoma* and the *réma*. Yet I find myself once again caught by this statement: *ming*, in Chinese, means at the same time 'to illuminate', 'brightness' and 'lucidity'. The great opposition established in our languages between the nominal and the verbal is erased. From that point, is the great open conflict between 'events' and 'things', in the way that our thought in Europe 'separates' them so that the former is abruptly detached from the latter, still pertinent?

From this point we can return once again to the path upon which we had embarked to try to go beyond the preconceptions in which, without even our thinking about it, language maintains us, and once more bring into play the Chinese divergence (*écart*), not on the basis that it offers an exotic window but in using it as a lever to move what has become immoveable within our philosophical questions and, still more, in their preconceptions. Because is not the characteristic of Chinese thought and, more generally, of what is called, using a very feeble word, 'wisdom' in relation to philosophy, precisely to dissolve the event? I believe that this exemplifies at once their coherence and power of seduction. It represents both a de-focusing and a de-dramatization (a de-contraction, if I dare call it this). Indeed, from what can it liberate us if not primarily from the emotion aroused by the event as it consumes our attention? The thought of 'silent transformations' logically ends in this as its result: the event is no longer anything but a continuous advent; it no longer constitutes a breaking into but becomes a matter of emergence. Instead of causing another possibility to appear, it is understood only as the consequence of such a subtle maturity that it has not ordinarily been possible to follow and observe.

Consequently, what constitutes possibility and what supports wisdom is no longer to be sought in the detachment of the exceptional and its 'additional factors' that are formed from the event in relation to the given but, rather, in the incidence of each 'moment', timely in its arrival and which we need to learn to welcome. In other words, first of all, to maintain equality with others, without privileging one moment or excepting it in relation to all moments, as true as it is that through its patent features there is already perceived—in a latent way—its coming reversal. Consequently, *every* moment is the right moment and it never ceases to teach wisdom, not simply as an occasion for virtue, *occasio virtulis*, calling for an effort on our part to confront it and rise to it (and so steel ourselves to it), as Stoicism demanded, but because every moment is 'in season', renewing itself in its other, and it legitimately alternates with others so that duration is deployed. The Sage, placing himself in phase with it, is such a 'seasonal' being (in the *Zuangzi*, 'Da zong shi', Guo Qingfan 1983: 230).

Attaching itself to the phenomena of transition that occurs at every moment, Chinese thought can only reach out in order to absorb the prestige of the event. Let us remember that ancient China did not compose an epic or a theatre, a staging of the event: it sacrificed its exceptionality for a constant *adaptation to the moment*. In returning to our preceding pairing: working for 'continuation', the 'modification', finding itself actively implicated in the evolution, is unable to detach itself, or still less to isolate itself, from it. For all that, does Chinese thought escape all rupture? Is it unaware of the danger? The better to demarcate them and be able to manage them, at the same time as to justify the ineradicable phenomenon of the 'casual encounter' (*shiran, ouran*), the Chinese have concentrated their attention on what they conceived as the tiny 'fuse' of change (the notion of *ji* in *The Book of Changes*) and which is precisely the initial state of modification, although the latter has barely been introduced, and that even as it is being outlined is not yet manifest. If there is a decisive moment, it is in this most 'subtle' state, examined by the Sage and the strategist, we are told, right at its 'depths': where, with the modification pointing towards the path to come, the unforeseeable blends opportunely with what is still undefined about the tendency, so that, with uncertainty thus fertilizing becoming, fresh germs of possibility appear. Having barely begun, the tendency which is engaged is carried through its own momentum to its deployment; and we will finally see it succeed, on a large scale, with the marvellous springing up of the 'event'.

Besides, how does one say 'event' in Chinese? To translate 'event' from the Western idea, modern Chinese says, 'fragment' or 'part' of the 'matter' (or the 'situation'): *shi-jian*. For example, the 'Events of Tiananmen' in 1989 were described as *Tian'an men shi-jian*. In other words, the dimension 'of fact', *pragma* in Greek, is not considered without taking into account, in parallel, what 'happens' (*to sumbebekos*), which befalls from it or is produced by it, as the Latin also says in *eventus* (in European languages: *event*, *evento* and even *Ereignis*?). If we consider the first encounter between these two worlds which were until then unaware of each other, we will understand how from that moment one of the main resistances to the entry of Christianity into China, in contrast with the assimilation of Buddhism a millennium earlier, was related precisely to this status of the Event as creating rupture. Because how, in a perspective of continuous unfolding as well as of renewal by means of alternation, could a place be found, indeed, for the idea of a radical event, admittedly one that is foretold but which resolutely cuts into the course of time and consequently demands Faith in order to integrate this impossibility?

Having ceaselessly prided themselves on the development of processes which, from the minuteness of their starting point, develop to the point of infinity, Chinese thought does not have to 'believe' in Rupture. It verifies this through the closest possible investigation, in all evolution. For example, let us consider health. While European medicine once more places its trust here and now in action, and is not afraid brutally to interrupt the course engaged upon (we 'operate', practice an 'intervention'), Chinese medicine has confidence in the capacity of indirect influence, by the diffuse, complete and long-term transformation of a remedy and a regime. Or again, one does not (suddenly) 'fall' sick, the adepts of the procedures of the 'Long life' tell us (testimony of Xi Kang 1990; see also Jullien 2007): such an event—the rupture—does not exist. It is simply produced from a disturbance, which starts very subtly until as it develops it suddenly one day crosses a threshold and becomes apparent. The brutality of the 'event' then amazes us, because we have not known how to distinguish the silent transformation which has imperceptibly led to it.

However, has not the reign of the event succeeded in imposing itself on the world based upon this double impact that monopolizes the attention and creates a dramatic tension? And this occurs everywhere... Communication has, without warning, succeeded where (religious) Conversion, in spite of its insistence, has struggled. What country, what culture, what distant place, including China, can still elude it? It is a reign, or rather a dictatorship, but the kind of dictatorship which is promoted these days: proximate, discreet and infiltrating, which cannot be delineated and against which we are still less able to resist—we do not dream of doing so. In the 'global' world, the media have really acquired, during these most recent decades, their ascendancy through a silent transformation, even one that is exemplary of its type. Is it not founded precisely on the successive—and stereotypical—fabrication of 'events'? It is not only the 'eventalization' by which they proceed which serves to capture the interest for them and, in so doing, to increase their audience and influence, but also, just as everything that Midas touches becomes gold, so everything the media speak about becomes an event. An event does not properly have to 'exist' and because of this it has eluded classic ontology: it is from the way in which it is arranged and treated, by which it succeeds in congealing around it the word and the spectacle, that it attains its consistency, or performance, of the event. In what way is the death of some singer, whose news circulates around France, playing on its pathos, more significant from the point of view of knowledge of the present than any other information that the development accorded to this death causes to be passed over in silence? And even—death for death—did the death of Deleuze (or of Ricoeur or Derrida) receive anything more than a brief announcement?

Televized News evidently exists in its ritual, which is no longer that of the everyday 'prayer' that Hegel wanted the Newspaper to become but an organized spectacle, and one that henceforth functions in the same way everywhere in the world, a simple montage of events. Should it be called Event-entertainment? Event-promotion, opening onto the unexpected through a new possibility, even if it is fictive, such as Christianity bore within it or as Badiou conceives it, is opposed to event-distraction, which television conveys and which has on the whole, as we know, not even been very informative. Its audience rating ('audimat') comes from elsewhere and stems primarily from its mixed format. Under cover of informing us, televized News supplies us with, not so much supports for fantasies, which would mean to recognize their legitimately fictional character, but what we will rather call 'pretexts' of actuality. It is an actuality theatre (as we would say a 'variety theatre'), since everything is done in it above all to suspend—fascinate—scandalize—recreate—and return to serenity, at least according to the usual scenario. We know that, as soon as an event is no longer prominent enough, when it has been exhausted from a dramatic point of view (in poignant resources) and its results are no longer adjudged sufficiently to link together intrigue and interest, then it will be removed from the screen and returned to obscurity. Yet it is precisely what such a fact, having occurred, entails in consequences that would be instructive: how the effects that have arisen stretch out from one day to the next and how the ordinary that gradually re-establishes itself diffuses and absorbs it, in short, into what silent transformation it has sunk.

To what extent has this phenomenon been contagiously extended? Through a silent transformation which moreover I do not see, and is also barely possible to analyze, so-called intellectual life is increasingly administered and formatted by the editing and consumption of events. Indeed, it passes into the hands of the 'event designers' who organize a 'philosophical event' in the same way as they do a marriage or a rally, one after the other—a new profession. Here too the event goes to market. Who is not aware that, in step with its commercial logic of monopolizing, which turns a book into a product like any other, even the 'launch' of a book is henceforth completely oriented in this direction? Now the event becomes an assault (at the same moment, all the media, the same formulae, the same photos, etc. I have seen the same piles of *Harry Potter* books in Beijing as in Paris . . .); then in no time the book is sold, consumed, sold out and forgotten, giving way to others and without even creating the trouble of leaving behind stock to manage—an operation that is beneficial in every way. More remarkable still, such use becoming prescriptive, books are today written in anticipation of the creation of an event. In France we have 'Shoah', 'May 68', 'the Beijing Olympics' and so on. Bookshop tables are covered with one and then with the other and the public head's is turned to one side and then to the other . . .

At the moment I am writing these lines, the news is breaking that Ingrid Betancourt[1] has been freed. Here at last is an event, one that is real, isolatable and demonstrable, expected and solid and not doubtful: on such a day, at such a time and in such a place, it really happened. There really was a Before and an After; there really is, diffused around the world, a communicative relief. And perhaps even this expectation and the preceding pressure, producing an increase in the power of the event, has allowed the event (even if I could also continue my analysis in this respect: it is thanks to the silent transformation by which the rebel forces have gradually grown weaker, with the capacity for initiative tipping over to the other side, that an operation could have been organized and have succeeded).

Nevertheless, every time this type of event is produced, even the most unquestionable and solidly based, such as a freeing of hostages, I am amazed at the way in which it is seized upon, consumed and drained of significance by the media. The event immediately plays at being an event . . . because the event 'consumes' itself. It consumes itself in order to put a little intensity into our lives, and we even revel in it. The pathos is immediately orchestrated, displayed and exhausted. We give ourselves the convenient impression, even the comfortable justification, that we are generously in tune with the world, although it is a matter only of an easy opportunity to shake off our apathy and finally to have something upon which to cling, to deal with, and to speak about. This effect of this fixation and monopolizing always surprises me as it causes everything else to be suddenly forgotten and produces this enlargement of a moment, one that is so soon destined to be wiped away.

I watch them both drinking peaceably from their glass, on the terrace, facing the sea, before going to dinner. The husband and the wife—they clearly have nothing to say to each other, and do not even expect to say anything. At what point do they find this unbearable? Their lifeless faces appear on the verge of suffocation: like two fishes cast onto the beach, out of their element, no longer having anything eventful, like the last trickle of running water, in which to save themselves. One can really verify, in this despair exposed to the point of indecency, what a metaphysical 'extension', to which we feverishly cling, the 'event' is. Now and then, shaking themselves a little, they ask a question, but without conviction or hope, apparently with such a lot of effort as though it was an enormous weight to be moved: 'Do you know if . . .' But this question is already given with no expectation of learning anything. They are desperately angling for a remnant of an event to give them a little of the fortuitous to move them or of intensity to lift them up. Admittedly the mobile phone is there at hand as a lifebuoy, but we have heard all those telephonic exchanges on the train from which, once the brief surprise of the call has passed, nothing is learned . . . Dazzled by this inexhaustible blueness which I will no longer see tomorrow and that I would so much like to capture, I would be ready to do anything to come to their aid: to cry wolf, or rather to upturn the table, so that there would finally be something for them which 'happens' that evening, something that 'takes place', offers a minimum for them to tell each other, and might allow them to breathe . . .

Note

1 Ingrid Betancourt, a Colombian politician kidnapped by the Revolutionary Armed Forces of Colombia (FARC) in 2002 and rescued in a Colombian military operation in 2008.—Trans.

Chapter 10
OF THE CONCEPT WHICH IS LACKING—
HISTORICAL-STRATEGIC-POLITICAL

I encountered the notion of 'silent transformation' in the corner of a page while reading the great contemplative work about History by the seventeenth century Chinese philosopher Wang Fuzhi: 'how will these unnoticed displacement(s)—the silent transformation(s) (*qian yi mo hua*)—one day be considered?' (1976, VOL. 2: 382). In this work, the notion is developed no further but it took root in the general thought of Wang Fuzhi. Let's take, for example, undoubtedly the most important mutation of Chinese history, the foundation of the Empire that took place in 221 BCE. This was the first empire in the world whose administrative structure took the place of feudalism—in comparison the Roman Empire, as it developed so carefully after the death of Caesar, seems a timid innovation, as witnessed by some of the rooms in the house of Caesar Octavius on the

Palatine Hill. The Chinese thinker applied himself to showing how this event, as decisive as any and constituting the most conspicuous rupture, in fact ensued from an in-depth orientation, or 'general propensity' (*da shi*), whose 'coherence' and rationality (the notion of *li*) could be examined. Admittedly, this unification of the Empire in violence and blood as well as this mutation of feudalism into bureaucracy, which was settled in an authoritarian way by the First Emperor, can appear to have effected a sudden revolution. Nevertheless, beneath the twists of History, a slower and more regular evolution, allowing the at once 'underlying' and 'logical' (*shi* and *li*) character of transformation to appear, can easily be discerned (I am referring to Jullien 1995).

This is revealed by the fact that, even before the First Emperor imposed this new form of authority, a number of territories which had lost their suzerainty, in the final centuries of Antiquity, had already passed under the tutelage of an administrative pattern: the new system therefore pre-existed the imperial resolution, which did no more than systematize it. On the other hand, hardly had this first dynasty dimmed than, less than twenty years later, those who had restored the Han returned to the system of fiefs: in other words, in addition to the bad memories left by the First Emperor, the promoter of reform, the ancient feudal system was still inscribed within habits and mentalities, and that the tendency which oriented the course of History could not support such a brutal change. But equally it could not, as our thinker tells us, really be a matter of turning back the clock. Those who were then afraid that the new masters of the Empire would, through the granting of grand fiefs, disturb their own power, and lead China back to the previous age of wars between principalities, 'lamented in vain', for want of understanding the inexorable (because 'logical') character of the evolution under way. Because it is clear that, once the power of the Han was consolidated, the revolts of the feudal princes, throughout the first century of the new dynasty, were condemned by their own nature to miscarry and no longer represented anything more than 'the last spark of a lamp on the point of going out': the granting of fiefs represented the 'last waves' of a dying world, and their quasi-abolition constituted the 'prelude' to the periods to come.

The event, as prominent as it appeared, was soon to be reabsorbed into what had come before as well as into what would come after: beforehand, its pre-figuration born of discreet maturations and, afterwards, one would long continue to trace the jolts resulting from the slow assimilation of the effected transformation. At the same time, the Chinese thinker was concerned to show that this transformation was universal: the passage from the fiefs to the prefectures presented not only an administrative and political interest but concerned the life of the people as a whole, and, first of all, in its material conditions. In this sense, even the domains which appear the least directly linked to this mutation—like the system of schools and the mode of selection—are nevertheless actively involved in such a modification. With all the institutions during this age becoming integrated and 'supporting each other mutually', it is this transformation of the whole, linking so many realms, that the historian was able to discern under all of its various aspects.

In Europe, we first learned History as children in a way that was dominated by events: the dates of the lives of kings, wars and treaties. For instance: Marignan: 1515.[1] As children in France we all learned this date: Marignan. Obviously Marignan is nothing. It was a pyrrhic victory—the entry of French troops into Italy principally gained the elegant châteaux which line the Loire. Then came Annales, and the teachings of Fernand Braudel juxtaposing this traditional narrative 'one would speak of a short time span, proportionate to individuals, to daily life . . .' a 'hasty' and dramatic recitative, with a new history whose research prioritized the great cyclical oscillations and laying stake on time periods (Braudel 1980: 28). Next to what Braudel called this 'explosive' and 'newly striking' event, of which the historian of the nineteenth century cast himself so willingly as director, while not disdaining, in order to capture the interest, to tweak the strings of suspense and emotion, henceforth extends this 'long' time or that 'gradual duration, this 'slow motion' time, drawn out over the centuries, as one has to consider it, for example, when studying mercantile capitalism from the fourteenth to the eighteenth century in Europe: a number of features are common and 'remain static' during these four centuries of economic life, maintaining an overall consistency in spite of spectacular changes and the multitude of events (however resonant!) which filled them.

Braudel therefore opposes short time to long time, the 'explosiveness' of the event on the one hand and a time so 'slowed down' that one finds oneself 'almost at the extreme of movement' on the other. This is because he remains caught, like all European historiography, in the imposed notion of *time becoming*, but as such, as we know, in a way external to physics whose fundamental modality is the narrative (it is really a matter, he says, of different 'recitatives'). But we are obliged to notice that Chinese historians, just like the philosophers of History in China, for whom God knows how important tradition is, have not developed their conceptions within a concept of 'time', for the very good reason that they did not possess one, at least not an explicit one, and that they rather thought in terms of continuous process—in terms of the Chinese *tao*. Has their work been handicapped for all that? For my part I would ask, as I advance prudently into this terrain which is not mine, if the notion of 'silent transformation' does not bear the great advantage of confirming the idea of 'long time' or of slow duration, as Braudel conceived it, when confronted with the short time of the event, without for all that falling into the contradiction of the 'immutable' and the 'moving', which the historian comes close to here and which we see remains to a great extent dependent on our metaphysics. When Braudel, making reference to anthropologists (Lévi-Strauss), rests his argument on notions of 'structure' or of 'models' in order to grasp the phenomenon of 'permanence' and regularity, it really appears as if the thought of non-change to which these notions infallibly lead work against what constitutes the very nature of History. But, as I have continually tried to show, the 'silence' (of History) is not immobility. This leads to the interest I see, for its unitary character, in the conception of a History conceived as a continual transformation whose 'underground displacements' are drawn out 'in silence', as Wang Fuzhi said, given their widespread nature, while the resounding *staccato* of events emerges from its surface and detaches itself, striking our attention.

The danger, on the other side, from a speculative point of view, as soon as one is freed of the dandruff of the event, is to start off again on a Hegelian (in fact, very broadly European) scenario governed by revelation and finality: to perceive a hidden progress under this chronological checking, like a hidden God, which would eventually manifest itself only retrospectively and afterwards from its surpassing; in short, once again to commit oneself perpetually to theodicy. The merit of the concept of silent transformation, in comparison, is that it sets us free from théo-téléological constructions and otherwise recomposes, in a non-metaphysical way, the relation between the visible and the invisible. Let us then reconfigure the relation between the two: transformation is gestation and stands for a condition; the event, as I have said, emerges on the surface. Because it is pervasive, operating in advance, at the stage of maturation, the transformation is always 'silent': and, because it detaches itself from it as it individualizes itself, the vent is the marker and the *index* of it.

The concept of silent transformation therefore not only avoids our having to separate what 'happens' from what carries it along (rather than what 'causes' it), or the chronological from what underlies it, but it also allows us to observe evolutions according to their orientation, without fastening them ideologically any longer to some expected Advent, and to examine the lines of force which are at work within them and the direction they are taking without pre-supposing a Meaning and a destination within the process. In other words, by no longer seeking some hypostasized Progress in History. This concept will moreover no longer allow History to be split up according to a difference of scale or domain, but for the histories of the 'greatest' and the 'smallest', the individual and the collective, and nature, the climate, species, people and each of them to be linked under its aegis. It comprises all of life and the slightest phenomenon, the erosion of mountains as well as the degeneration of cells; equally what appears to be an affection and turns it into indifference, without even being noticed, or what from one day to the next cracks open dictatorships and, spreading out in silence, one fine day advances belief in the possibility of Revolution and their overthrow.

If appropriate to the study of History, would the concept of silent transformation not equally be so for an analysis of the present? From what is France today (in the spring-summer of 2008) constituted? Is it made from the politicians' 'buzzwords', upon which the Media comment as 'events' over and over again, furnishing the news from one day to the next, but which are forgotten immediately afterwards? These obviously represent nothing but lines of foam. Are they the measures, for example of reform, which would be adopted? But they only exist after the discreet ripening of so many general conditions which have made them possible. A slow erosion has undermined a whole, previously untouchable, ideological edifice which one believed to be so much more formidable, but that we see gradually breaking down, piece by piece, like pasteboard, or arousing only a little resistance from a rearguard, acknowledged and become artificial. Even the Berlin Wall came down due to an erosion and inertia characteristic of the system. Each age in its turn repeats, as though for the first time, what

Hegel says of his own, as if in echo of the Chinese thinker, distinguishing between what 'ripens slowly and silently', *langsam und still*, and what 'dissolves bit by bit' the ancient edifice: 'whose tottering state is only hinted at by isolated symptoms. The frivolity and boredom which unsettle the established order, the vague foreboding of something unknown, these are the heralds of approaching change' (Hegel 1977: 6-7).

Or is it elections which constitute present-day politics in a periodic way and which are mounted through the media and experienced as the great Event, that guide the years to come and are even decided, we are promised, by 'society's choice'? But it is not difficult to see that they are themselves the fruit of long term inflexions that give birth to progressive reversals which from afar and in advance order the result. They conspicuously and even theatrically proclaim a Rupture, but how long will it take before this media hype is reabsorbed? At the very most, elections ratify the mutations which nurture, or precipitate, the evolution in progress by rendering them distinct. The myth of humans as being able to choose-act is necessary to democracy, and is thus salutary to preserve, but it cannot hide what it detaches itself from: it could not conceal the importance of what is neither the weight of structures nor anonymous forces, that have traditionally been opposed to it, but these *general orientations* and *discreet propensities* (*da shi*, the Chinese say) inflecting their epoch. In the last presidential election in France (2007), I especially remember how it brought to the surface in a manifest, and even spectacular, way, with a new threshold being crossed, the surrounding mediatization that I have begun to evoke by virtue of a fundamental, silent, transformation, gradually reconfiguring public space in its entirety, during these last decades (in this case, of course, I am making a contrast between the public and the media circus), and thereby contaminating it through consumption of the sensational and putting into the limelight 'personalities', even their private lives, *stars* or *celebrities*, not only in the political field but in that of the judiciary or of intellectual life.

Who will now take stock of the silent but profound transformation of intellectual life in France (in Europe?) today? Without our having been alert to it, the figure of the intellectual has, in the course of the years, been split into two like an amoeba. This has generated, on the one hand, the philosophy of opinion, which chooses a role (even a garb) and displays it in an easily identified 'posture', gets involved on every stage and gives its opinion about every argument, indeed goes as far as to pass off the excessiveness of its position (which is so easy for the media to consume) as a theoretical radicalism. An ostensible giver of lessons, it surfs over the conformism and ideological correctness of the day with all the more success for playing inexhaustibly upon Revolt, to which it initially lays claim in the name of 'non-conformism' and being 'in-correct'. The criteria retained are no longer ones of notoriety, an outmoded term referring back to recognition of merit or competence but of exposure and 'visibility'. Next to this, what is inevitably relegated into the shadows, because it is not spectacular, is the philosophy that could be said to be about 'elaboration', in other words that works from questions and produces concepts. This is a position all the more in retreat because, in the bookshops, on the other bank, it also sees its place shrink, from year to year and from shelf to shelf, to the benefit of the flourishing genres of *zen*, 'well-being' and 'personal development' (in the form of non-books) that prosper from the renunciation of any construction in thought. Between these two processes, its profit margin (its public) is reduced from one day to the next—but who speaks about this 'underground displacement' and who will even realize it is taking place?

Or then again, among so many other correlated symptoms, reacting more and more massively to fashion (i.e. to what has already been said and can easily capture the interest), the literary supplements of newspapers are shrinking like shagreen skin before our eyes, frittering away their articles and no longer daring to deal with 'difficult' books. In the name, they say, of non-elitism, of more democracy and accessibility (only History is still spared). This means that publishers are less and less inclined to publish such books, because they are too demanding, or they publish them sparingly, so as to maintain their image, 'so as not to not . . .' and so on. An insidious and global transformation, once more, from which we will one day brutally awaken and measure its results—just as one looks at a photograph of oneself from twenty years earlier. Here is what has become impossible to imagine: on the one hand, Julien Gracq writing his novels without any regard for the press or, on the other hand, Roland Barthes publishing his *Mythologies* in a weekly newspaper.

No longer to envisage, no longer to dare (the recession) is a typical symptom of silent transformations—in its capacity to manifest, a *symptom* signifies, following its etymology, the dimension of ramification and conjunction of what is hidden while an *index*, in contrast, signifies the capacity to detach oneself; that is characteristic of what promotes itself as a sign. No longer to dare to run (or even to think about it) or to bathe in cold seas, is a symptom of ageing-renunciation. Or else it is what we no longer envisage (no longer imagine) saying to the other, what we gradually keep to ourselves without even being alert to the fact, and which returns us to silence, and that, as on a barometer, measures the general decline of a love in the process of unravelling. Whether we withdraw the vital energy, or the confidence in the other, into ourselves, there is hardly anything left from which to expect a directly positive sign that would be salient and interesting: this is not event but erosion. Such a retreat is not advertised, and it is entirely the *situational* which is globally implicated in it: an accumulation or a negative secretion is thereby solidified from one day to the next and erects a wall that is increasingly opaque and massive even though invisible, and which gradually separates us from the old possibilities and causes them to retreat indefinitely and then be forgotten. This is also true in the political sphere: is it not the *narrowing of possibilities* (which means that no one any longer dares, no longer envisages, and is not even amazed by the fact) that ought to pre-occupy the leaders in France today, rather than the invoking of one or another cause of an attributable malaise?

Confronted with which the concept of silent transformation presents another problem: can one have a hold over it (although it is antinomic to action) instead of allowing oneself to be reduced by it to passivity? As a descriptive concept, could the silent transformation become an art of managing? In other words, could one make a concept from the silent transformations which would be strategic, and even a political vocation? In this way to turn the concept of silent transformation into a concept of behaviour would imply thinking not only about what, at an antagonistic level, a practice of *erosion* and a gradual exhaustion of the adversary can be, but also, more generally and in a positive way, of what can be a form of management by *induction*. Rather than claim to project its action immediately over the course of things and to impose itself upon it, to 'induce', means to know how to engage with a process discreetly, from afar, but in such a way that it would be carried by its own momentum to develop, and that, as it infiltrates the situation, it will gradually succeed, and without one even taking account of it, in silently transforming it. This amounts to envisaging, in the face of the powers of *modelling*, whose inconsistent effects we are aware of in science and which have guaranteed the technical success of the modern West, what an art of *maturation* would be.

A common way of approaching efficacy, which Greek philosophy developed on a grand scale, is to conceive of an ideal form (*eidos*) representing a duty-to-be, from which a plan is made, in other words put forward as an aim (*telos*), and which serves as a model of the paradigm (as Plato described in an exemplary way). And this applies even to war: in troop movements as much as in the course of battle, a general is more or less skilful depending, as Plato tells us, on whether he had 'studied geometry [and] would be a very different person from what he would be if he had not' (*The Republic*; 1961e, 526d: 759)—geometry being henceforth, in the West, the model of the model (and mathematics the *language* in which this model is written). Finding itself called upon at the same time by the two queens of the faculties which are, in European psychology, on the one hand understanding, which conceives 'with a view towards the better' (the ideal form), and on the other hand the will which is then invested to make this conform with reality, with everything this 'conformity' implies of compulsion. This has resulted in the theory-practice relation, so common that we barely question it, even if we always dread some excess of 'practice', at the stage of 'action', in relation to the theory and the model it has projected.

But another way of conceiving efficacy, which we read notably in the *Art of War* of ancient China, is not to reconfigure the situation in an ideal way, in which a plan is made and an aim set up, but to ripen the conditions encountered, even the very ones in which one is oneself implicated. In other words, to transform silently the situation engaged with in such a way that it progressively inclines in a favourable direction and that this gradual inflection, forming a gradient, will cause the effects to come tumbling down by themselves, therefore indirectly of any desired end: as tiny as the favourable factors located in the heart of the situation might initially be, whoever knows how to propagate them will be able to make the 'potential of the situation' tip over onto his side (see the notion of *shi*, the same character I explained earlier as the orienting tendency of the course of History). Let us recall these maxims of Sun Zi: If the enemy is relaxed, one may make him fatigued; if he is full, one may make him hungry; if he is settled, one may make him move. Without his even being able to account for it, you will have transformed him to such an extent that he might lose the capacity to resist you; from that point you hardly need to attack him because he will have defeated himself and 'action' will be unnecessary.

I have drawn this strategic notion of *maturation* in particular from an anecdote reported in the *Mencius*: a peasant, who wants his wheat to grow, pulls on the shoots; in the evening, when his children race to see the results, everything has dried up (1963: 78).[2] By pulling on the shoots, aiming directly at the effect through this action, he forced things and inevitably produced the opposite effect to that intended. The development is contained in the situation: the seed is in the earth and asks only to grow. Should he therefore stand passively at the side of the field and watch it grow, telling himself: I expect the wheat will grow . . . No, of course not. He ought, Mencius tells us, simply to do what any peasant knows, which is discreet and not heroic, i.e. from one day to the next, to hoe, weed and turn the earth around the shoots—to promote the growth, in other words to encourage the silent transformation which will gradually succeed before our eyes but without our being able to see it. One day the wheat will be ripe and it will only be necessary to cut it. Aid what emerges on its own, echoes the *Tao te Ching* (Lao-tzu 1992, § 64: 48 [*Yi fu wan wu zhi ziran*]), upsetting our Greek opposition between the natural and the mechanical (*phusis/techne*). China, a land of agriculturalists and not of pastoralists, having no awareness of God leading his flock by means of the word and conversing with it, has always meditated on the silent maturing of the effect. It defied the Word just as much as it did Action, because both appeared equally to involve a forced intervention. The Sage (Confucius) did not even teach his disciples. He did not give lessons, and delivered no Message to them: he was content with prompting them, from one day to the next, by means of brief indications given to each one according to his situation, as so many finishing touches, or pushes on the spade, so as to allow wisdom to ripen within them (I am referring to Jullien 2000, Chapter 9).

This strategy, by which *inducing the effect* is the opposite of ordering it from without, in which ripening responds to erosion, both of which occur quietly and are extended in duration, in a way that is more efficient than spectacular and does not emphasize the Self-Subject (i.e. conceiving and wanting something which is then verified on the basis of a military plan). As an illustration of this clash of strategies, was not the battle of Dien Bien Phu (if this really was a 'battle') the result of such a capacity to exploit and ripen the conditions favourable to exhausting the adversary? Or take Deng Xiaoping, 'the little Helmsman', who was, if I may call him this, the 'silent transformer' of China: advancing step by step, or 'stone by stone', as he said, rather than by projecting some plan or model, but for all that doing so without falling back into the empiricism (pragmatism) which is the other side of the coin of our idealism: since it was a question here more of attaching oneself obstinately to the concrete, of making good use of propensities at work, for the duration, as much as of the capacity for self-deployment of the process.

This has worked so well that China, we note retrospectively today, has been able to reverse completely its social and economic system by continuous transition, leaving the regime and the Party in place but profoundly transformed (compare this with the USSR becoming Russia again as it passed through so many successive ruptures: the Twentieth Congress, de-Khrushchevization, Perestroika and so on). Even 'de-Maoization' did not involve the tearing down of Mao's statue, but the prudently governed silent transformation of the figure of the Great Helmsman (the leader of the Revolution as the founder of a new Empire). And the Olympic Games of 2008 represented the henceforth visible and even spectacular surface emergence from the potential of a situation which has constantly increased during these past few decades, by making good use of all the conditions or rivalries favourable to it and without any great events. Or you can see it as the Chinese quarter in Paris silently spreads out and slowly extends without our speaking about it, without it even occurring to us to be amazed by it... Whoever studies the tactic of enveloping in the game of Go in comparison with the frontality of the game of chess will easily understand its importance by learning not to destroy the adversary but to control as much territory as possible by constructing networks while extending out from them through an entanglement which increasingly tightens its influence. I do not believe, in short, that one can understand China, including its history and contemporary politics, without passing through the coherences and categories it has developed that stand apart from heroism and action and the projection of a plan of ideas.

Does this mean that this strategy of silent transformations is the prerogative of one culture and reserved for it alone? I would challenge such a culturist point of view just as much as I would our easy universalism since we in Europe are not excluded from these coherences, even if they have not there been conceptually exploited in our tradition—all that is necessary is patience (there is no Chinese 'inscrutability' here), just as we can verify them through our own experience. The gain, as we encounter external thinking, is rather one of intelligibility, to the extent that this detour allows us finally to risk the overturning of our concepts while going back to look at what our theoretical tools have left obscure or unilluminated. It will be recalled that, during the first period of cohabitation (1986–88), President François Mitterrand, without advancing, knew how to make good use of each occasion over the two years in such a way as silently to erode the position of his adversary, causing him to expend himself, to force his action and consequently to weaken himself, to the point that the situation may be progressively turned against him ('time has to be given time', according to his formula). It has been said of Mitterrand that he was 'Florentine' (Machiavellian). Is this the most appropriate notion?

To pass from a strategic use of the concept of silent transformation to its political vocation, a change of scale, the Chinese tell us, will be sufficient: this transformation should no longer be put to work for individual advantage, by undermining the position of the adversary so as to cause power to turn in one's favour (in which Mao also engaged in at the beginning of the Cultural Revolution), but of deploying it more fully to the world's profit. 'Profit' (*li*) is too restricted a word to express it. The Chinese character represents an ear of wheat bordered by the blade to cut it: good politics allows conditions to ripen so that the fruits can be harvested for the whole community, in a rounded manner, without any longer aiming at them but by virtue of the results (notions of *ben* opposed to *mo*), and thus without even dreaming of taking pride in doing so. This would imply having done with the reactivity in events as much as with the upheavals of reality in order to respond to modifications, when they have barely been sketched out, in a way so as to anticipate the danger they represent, since it is only embryonic and easy to reduce; or rather to favour its deployment across duration, in the long term, when it turns to common advantage. In other words, in both cases, to intervene directly beforehand, *at the level of conditions*, in order to inflect the situation in the desired direction, and not later, in the spectacular form of action and the urgency of reparations. Therefore one should not promise an ostensible success within a hundred days, but in some way to make the potential return, that the situation will produce rewards, that the 'indicators' will begin to reverse and confidence will reappear of its own volition.

From these consistencies, which can be seen to have been woven indefinitely into ancient China, from one realm to another, and never criticized, which amaze no one, about which they would not even dream of being amazed, will be definitively drawn not some reverie about the 'Tao' but a tool. Yet this concept of silent transformations will never (should I admit it?) become a concept as we might desire it to be: brilliant, intense, cut up clearly by the intelligence and like lightning in the sky of ideas. It does not respond to an enigma or free us from any contradiction; it is neither inventive nor combative; it makes no appeal to the heroism of thought. Could I describe it as a concept of wisdom rather than a philosophy? It will remain in the image of what it thinks: decanting progressively into the mind, as the days go by, with the advance of age, when the decline comes and recapitulations begin. It therefore inserts itself discretely into thought *without our thinking about it.* But equally it no more allows us to cast it aside once one has located it and has criticized all other concepts.

This concept which is lacking is the one *which remains*, in short, a 'fundamental' concept in avoiding the *a priori* of the others: since it takes advantage of no rupture, not even with the event (which it makes its emergence). Since it excludes nothing and is unpolemical, since 'Being', in comparison, *Sein* or *Être*, is after all only a Greek choice of value especially in response to the problems of definition as well as to the demands of the determination of science: a concept which promotes, but by means of exclusion (of non-being and even of appearance), obstructs the intelligence of the transition and relegates 'becoming' into the inconsistency of our lives. Or since 'reality', 'real', *'réel'*, is only a desperately flat concept, dejected, inert, unsatisfactory and disillusioned and which is still tied naively, secretly, to the 'thing', to the *res*: the most neutral concept, one might say, but with a false neutrality, since it sends us back into the 'unreal', through resignation, the dream, the pleasure principle and the figurations of the ideal.

As soon as we give up the monopolizing of events and thus untie the fixations of language; when we break the ordinary, quasi fixed, distance we maintain with what we see and live and, varying the field of focus, distance ourselves from it or come closer to it—what remains, in fact? What else is there still right in front of us but the grass which grows and the mountains which erode, bodies which become heavy and faces which become emaciated, life which fecundates, or becomes exhausted, or rather which, while fecundating, is already starting to become exhausted? And vague expectations that crystallize into feverish passion, or else meetings that become less frequent. Or amorous complicities which, without being confessed, turn into relations of power? Or heroic revolutions which (without our being about to locate when) mutate into the privileges of the Party? Or else the wounds of yesterday which are displaced, buried and condensed, and then transcribe themselves into encrypted representation of dreams—and works which ripen in silence?

Do we even know from where we have taken these fundamental terms which direct our thought or when they were born? They did not arise from the decision of a philosopher, but were given birth in the shadows by centuries of almost anonymous thought from which have gradually emerged new structures which we then believe are 'evidently' essential to us and can serve as a necessary foundation of the Truth. How many centuries of silent transformations have been necessary for the 'subject', that substrate of change, to be able finally to mean the subject of subjectivity; or the 'object', confronted with it, the objectivity of science and so on. These terms have rather undergone so many gradual inflections, to the point of being turned on their heads, to the extent that, from man belonging to the 'people' of God, the *laos* of the *Septante*, is gradually born its contrary, the 'lay' of the 'laity'. Have we ever thought otherwise than through silent transformation from whose surface suddenly emerges some clear thought, creating an 'event', which then resounds and mobilizes? Has one never seen anything but energies which are condensed and suns which consume themselves? With, now and then, resonant revelations of this uninterrupted weaving, on which we have out eyes wide open without sufficiently noticing anything in it, a world which falls and dies, a star which suddenly explodes.

Notes

1. At Marignan, near Milan, the French defeated the Swiss in 1515. —Trans.
2. In the English translation they are rice plants, not wheat.—Trans.

BIBLIOGRAPHY

Translator's Note

Translations into English of the Chinese classics referred to, where they exist, often bear little relation with the French translation as quoted by the author. This is especially the case for the *Book of Changes*, the *I Ching* or the *Yi Jing*. We have therefore drawn upon existing translations where this seemed appropriate and otherwise have translated from the French text. References are therefore given both to available English translations and the French translations given by the author. Where texts have not been translated into French, the Chinese originals are given. In these cases, we have translated from the author's translations into French.

AESCHYLUS. 1956. *Agamemnon* in *The Orestian Trilogy* (Philip Vellacott trans.). Harmondsworth: Penguin.

ARISTOTLE. 1984a. *Physics* in the *Complete Works of Aristotle*, VOL 1 (Jonathan Barnes trans. and ed.). Princeton, NJ: Princeton University Press.

———. 1984b. *Metaphysics* in the *Complete Works of Aristotle*, VOL. 2 (Jonathan Barnes trans. and ed.). Princeton, NJ: Princeton University Press.

BADIOU, Alain. 2000. *Ethics: An Essay on the Understanding of Evil* (Peter Hallward trans.). London & New York: Verso.

———. 2003. *Saint Paul: The Foundation of Universalism* (Ray Brassier trans.). Stanford: Stanford University Press.

———. 2005. *Being and Event* (Oliver Feltham trans.). New York: Continuum.

BAUDELAIRE, Charles. 1993. *The Flowers of Evil* (James McGowan trans.). Oxford: Oxford University Press.

BERGSON, Henri. 1984. *La Pensée et le mouvant* in *Oeuvres*. Paris: Presses Universitaires de France.

BRAUDEL, Fernand (1980) 'History and the Social Sciences: the *longue durée*' in *On History* (Sarah Matthews trans.). Chicago: University of Chicago Press.

Chuang tzu. 1992. In *The Essential Tao* (Thomas Cleary trans. and ed.). New Jersey: Castle Books.

DIELS-KRANTZ. 1952. *Die Fragmente der Vorsokratiker* (Walther Kranz rev.). Berlin: Weidmann.

DOUGLAS, Alfred. 1971. *The Oracle of Change: How to Consult the I Ching*. Harmondsworth: Penguin.

FRÄNKEL, Hermann. 1966. *Wege und Formen frühgriechischen Denkens. Literarische und philosophiegeschichtliche Studien*. Munich: Beck.

FREUD, Sigmund. 1977. 'On the Universal Tendency to Debasement in the Sphere of Love' in *On Sexuality*, (James Strachley trans.; Angela Richards comp. and ed.). Harmondsworth: Penguin.

———. 1984. 'Instincts and their Vicissitudes' (1915) in *On Metapsychology: The Theory of Psychoanalysis* (James Strachey trans.; Angela Richards comp. and ed.). Harmondsworth: Penguin.

GRAHAM, A. C. 1978. *Late Mohist Logic, Ethics and Science*. Cambridge & London: Cambridge University Press and SOAS.

GREEN, André. 1999. *The Work of the Negative*. London: Free Association Books.

GUO Qingfan (ed). 1983. *Xiaozheng Zhuangzi*. Taipei: Shijie shuju.

HARBSMEIER, Christoph. 1995. 'Some Notions of Time and of History in China and in the West with a Digression on the Anthropology of Writing' in Chun-chieh Huang and Eric Zürcher (eds), *Time and Space*. Leidon: Brill.

HEGEL, Georg Wilhelm Friedrich. 1969. *Science of Logic* (A. V. Miller trans.). London: George Allen & Unwin

———. 1977. *Phenomenology of Spirit* (A. V. Miller trans., with analysis of the text and foreword by J. N. Findlay). Oxford: Clarendon Press.

HERACLITUS of Ephesus. 2000. *Fragments* (Robin Waterfield trans. and ed.) in *The First Philosophers: The pre-Socratics and the Sophists*. Oxford: Oxford University Press.

HYPPOLITE, Jean. 1974. *Genesis and Structure of Hegel's 'Phenomenology of Spirit'*. Evanson, IL: Northwestern University Press.

I Ching, or, Book of Changes. 1968. The Richard Wilhelm translation. Rendered into English by Cary F. Baynes. London: Routledge & Kegan Paul.

Jullien, François. 1993. *Figures de immanence. Pour un lecture philosophique du 'Yi Jing'*. Paris: Grasset.

———. 1995. *The Propensity of Things: Toward a History of Efficacy in China*. (Janet Lloyd trans.). Brooklyn: Zone Books.

———. 2000. *Detour and Access: Strategies of Meaning in China and Greece* (Sophie Hawkes trans.). Brooklyn: Zone Books.

———. 2001. *Du 'temps', éléments d'une philosophie de vivre*. Paris: Grasset.

———. 2003. *Le valeur allusive*. Paris: Presses universitaires de France.

———. 2004. *A Treatise on Efficacy: between Western and Chinese Thinking*. Honolulu: University of Hawai'i Press.

———. 2006. *Si parler va sans dire. Du logos et autres resources*. Paris: Éditions de Seuil.

———. 2007. *Vital Nourishment: departing from happiness* (Arthur Goldhammer trans.). Brooklyn: Zone Books.

———. 2008. *De l'universel, de l'uniforme, du commune et du dialogue entre les cultures*. Paris: Fayard (forthcoming in 2011 as *The Universal, the Uniform and the Common: Dialogue between Cultures*. Oxford: Polity Press).

Klein, Étienne. 2007. *Le Facteur temps ne sonne jamais deux fois*. Paris: Flammarion.

Lao-tzu. 1992. *Tao te Ching* in *The Essential Tao* (Thomas Cleary trans. and ed.). New Jersey: Castle Books.

Maupassant, Guy de. 1970. 'Farewell' in *The Complete Short Stories*, vol. 2, London: Cassell.

Mencius. 1963. A new translation arranged and annotated for the general reader by W. A. C. H. Dobson. London: Oxford University Press.

MONTAIGNE, Michel de. 1987. *The Essays* (M. A. Screech trans.). Harmondsworth: Penguin.

ONIANS, Richard Broxton. 1973. *The Origins of European Thought*. New York: Arno Press.

PASCAL, Blaise. 1966. *Pensées* (A. J. Krailsheimer trans.). Harmondsworth: Penguin.

PLATO (1961a) *Parmenides* (F. M. Crawford trans.) in *The Collected Dialogues of Plato* (Edith Hamilton and Huntington Cairns eds). Princeton: Princeton University Press.

———. 1961b. *Phaedo* (Hugh Tredernich trans.) in *The Collected Dialogues of Plato* (Edith Hamilton and Huntington Cairns eds). Princeton: Princeton University Press.

———. 1961c. *The Sophist* (F. M. Crawford trans.) in *The Collected Dialogues of Plato* (Edith Hamilton and Huntington Cairns eds). Princeton: Princeton University Press.

———. 1961d. *Theaetetus* (F. M. Crawford trans.) in *The Collected Dialogues of Plato* (Edith Hamilton and Huntington Cairns eds). Princeton: Princeton University Press.

———. 1961e. *The Republic* (Paul Shorey trans.) in *The Collected Dialogues of Plato* (Edith Hamilton and Huntington Cairns eds). Princeton: Princeton University Press.

PLOTINUS. 1992. *The Enneads* (Stephen McKenna trans.). New York: Larsen Publications.

PROUST, Marcel. 1981a. *In Search of Lost Time, Volume V*: 'The Captive' (C. K. Scott Moncrieff and Terence Kilmartin trans., D. J. Enright rev.). London: Chatto & Windus.

———. 1981b. *In Search of Lost Time, Volume VI*: 'Time Regained' (Andreas Mayo and Terence Kilmartin trans., D. J. Enright rev.). London: Chatto & Windus.

Romano, Claude. 1998. *L'Événement et le monde*. Paris: Presses Universitaires de France.

Romilly, Jacqueline de. 1971. *Le temps dans la tragédie grecque*. Paris: Vrin.

Sophocles. 1982. *Oedipus at Colon* (Robert Eagles trans.) in *The Three Theban Plays*. Harmondsworth: Penguin.

———. 2007. *Ajax* (Peter Meineck and Paul Woolruff trans.) in *Four Tragedies*. Indianapolis: Hackett.

Sun Tzu. 2005. *The Art of War* (John Minford trans.). London: Penguin.

Tchouang-tse. 1973. *L'oeuvre complete de Tchouang-tse* (Liou Kia-hway trans.). Paris: Gallimard.

Tolstoy, Leo (2003) *Anna Karenina: a Novel in Eight Parts* (Richard Pevear and Larissa Volokhonsky trans.; with a preface by John Bayley). London: Penguin.

Wang Fuzhi. 1976. *Dutongjianlun*. Beijing: Zhong hua shuju.

Wu Kuang-ming. 1998. 'Time in China' in *On the 'Logic' of Togetherness: a Cultural Hermeneutics*. Leiden: Brill.

Xi Kang. 1990. *Yang sheng lun* (Essay on Nourishing Life) Shanghai: Shanghai gu jichu ban she.

Zhongyong. 2001. *Focusing the Familiar: A Translation and Philosophical Interpretation of the Zhongyong* (Roger T. Ames and David L. Hall trans. and annot.). Honolulu: University of Hawaii Press. Chinese text available at: ctext.org/liji/zhong-yong

INDEX

Aeschylus 108
Anaximander 108, 111, 114
Aristotle 18-20, 30, 32, 35-8, 40, 42-3, 53, 54-5, 70, 86, 91, 103, 105-06, 109
Badiou, Alain 122-3, 131
Barthes, Roland 147
Baudelaire, Charles 50, 51, 111
Bergson, Henri 41-2, 52
Betancourt, Ingrid 133, 135n
Braudel, Fernand 139-41
Chuang tzu 46
Chuang tzu 61
Clausewitz, Karl von 63
Confucius 152
Deleuze, Gilles 131
Derrida, Jacques 131
Deng Xiaoping 152-3
Fraenkel, Hermann 107
Freud, Sigmund 77, 84
Gracq, Julien 147
Harbsmeier, Christoph 103

Hegel, Georg Wilhelm Friedrich 30, 90, 91-2, 93-4, 131, 141, 144
Heidegger, Martin 54, 57, 112
Heraclitus 90-1
Hesiod 106
Book of Changes (*Yi Jing* or *I Ching*) 21-2, 24n, 70-01, 73-4, 76, 79, 82-3, 84, 87, 111, 128
Homer 106, 122
Klein, Étienne 115
Lao tze 48
Lao Tzu 33, 35, 39, 151
Mao Zedong 153, 155
Maupassant, Guy de 62
Mencius 151
Mencius 151
Mitterrand, François 154-5
Montaigne, Michel de 60, 112
Onians, Richard Broxton 106

Parmenides 58
Pascal, Blaise 13–14, 110
Pindar 107
Plato 17-19, 19-20, 30, 31–2, 35, 40, 43–4, 46, 62, 81, 84–6, 93, 104, 149
Plotinus 104, 111–12
Proust, Marcel 2, 4, 56, 63, 110, 112–13, 116–17
Ricoeur, Paul 131

Romano, Claude 124
Ronsard, Pierre de 110
Sophocles 108, 111
Stendhal, 63
Sun Zi 150
Tolstoy, Leo 63–4, 118
Wang Fuzhi 136, 141
Wu Kuang-ming 103
Xi Kang 129
Zhongyong 10, 44, 45, 79